HOW TO SERVE A VIP:

30 TIPS TO EARN & RE-EARN YOUR CUSTOMERS' LOYALTY

Dr. Bryan K. Williams
KEYNOTE SPEAKER • AUTHOR • CONSULTANT

★ ★ ★ ★ ★

B. Williams Enterprise, LLC

★ ★ ★ ★ ★

We exist to serve others so they may better serve the world. ®

www.bwenterprise.net

info@bwenterprise.net

ENTERPRISE
Customer Service
Training • Consulting • Products

Contents

A Message from the Author

Serving. Giving. Sharing. Teaching. To me, they all mean the same thing. I love to use the knowledge and resources I've been blessed with to bless others. No matter who they are. That is the true purpose of this book. In most people's minds, the VIP's are the people whom you treat with extra special care and attention. They get the absolute best version of you…all the time. If no one else gets a smile, you make sure that the VIP gets the biggest smile in the history of forever!

The assumption in this book, however, is that everyone we serve is a VIP. Specifically, we are not trying to treat VIP's like everyone else. Instead, we are treating everyone like they are VIP's. This assertion is a paradigm shift that may make some people uncomfortable, because it assumes that everyone is worthy of being served with excellence. If you believe that, then this book will help affirm your belief in service excellence, and memorable experiences.

-Bryan

This book is dedicated to my amazing family whom I love unconditionally...Lisa, Brylee & Bali.

1. Be Eager to Serve

Have you ever walked into a business and left before you were served? That scenario has happened to me multiple times. On past occasions, I left because the staff showed no sense of urgency to be of service. Please note that the business(s) had the product or service I wanted, but I left because there was an obvious sense of apathy among the staff. Yes, your customers can feel the apathy; especially if the majority of the staff look like they would much rather be anywhere else besides work.

> *"...I left because there was an obvious sense of apathy among the staff."*

Example 1:

I was at a hotel recently and getting ready to check out. I had two bags with me and while approaching the front desk, I saw the front desk agent and the bellman casually talking. I could tell it was a casual conversation based on their postures. The agent was slouched over the desk, the bellman was leaning on the desk with one elbow, and his feet were crossed. I know that co-workers are often times good friends so casual conversations amongst the staff are to be expected. However, if a customer approaches, PLEASE stop the chit-chat, assume a professional posture, give eye-contact, smile, and welcome the customers as though you have been waiting just for them all day. So as I approached the desk, the front desk agent and bellman continued to chat.

Even when I actually got to the desk and looking both of them in their eyes, there was still no change. I (the guest) had to be the one to say "Good Morning". **[Note: If your customer has to acknowledge you first, then you have failed.]** Being eager to serve shows that you hardly can wait to serve your customers, and it shows in your eye contact, tone of voice, and overall body language.

Example 2:

The phenomena of the customer being the first one to give a greeting is more common than you may think. On a recent trip to the shopping mall, I decided to keep track of how many times I said "hello" or "good afternoon" before the store attendant did. Each time, I waited until the attendant saw me, then waited at least 25 seconds while I was directly in front of the attendant. In other words, I gave ample opportunity for the attendants to greet me first. On three different occasions within a 30-minute span, I was the one who had to say hello first in order for someone to acknowledge that I was in their store and needed assistance. Not good.

Example 3:

On a recent trip to Texas, I was on my way to pick up my rental car at the Austin International Airport. As I was walking to the Enterprise Rent-A-Car parking lot, I noticed one of the employees walking towards my direction. I thought he was going to the airport terminal where I just came from. As it turns out, he was actually walking towards me to greet me! He met me halfway between where I was and the rental car booth. That rental car agent was eager to serve.

*"...being eager to serve means that you are **constantly** looking for ways to engage your customers."*

Many people believe that the greeting is the first step of service, when in fact, being eager to serve happens before the greeting. Being eager to serve means that you are **constantly** looking for ways to engage your customers. Many of you reading this have heard of the ***10 feet / 4 feet rule*** (or 3 meters / 1.2 meters). Basically, if a customer is within 10 feet of you, give eye contact, smile...(at the very least, acknowledge that the customer is alive!). If you are within 4 feet, then you initiate dialogue, offer assistance, etc. So if you are in an elevator and a customer comes into the same elevator, you are automatically within the 4-feet rule. This means, you are not allowed to look down at the floor or look at the elevator numbers passing by, hoping that your floor comes soon (so you won't have to speak). I have seen that transpire many times also.

The purpose of being eager to serve is to show your customers that there is nothing more important, at that moment, than serving them. Your actions should say, *I am at your service*. So, instead of walking out of a business because of the apathetic staff, the eagerness of the team should pique your interest and have you wondering, "WOW, I can't wait to experience the rest of the service". If your goal is to create an exceptional experience for your customers, then you must be attentive…be hospitable…be memorable, and above all, be eager to serve.

"…show your customers that there is nothing more important, at that moment, than serving them."

Activity – Be Eager to Serve

1. With input from your team and customers, develop standards that clearly articulates your expectations on "being eager to serve". For example:

   a. We will answer the phone within three rings and a smile

   b. If someone is within 4 feet (1.2 meters), we will proactively approach the customer and offer assistance

   c. Reply to emails by the end of the business day

   d. Greet others with a smile, whether in a person or on the phone

   e. Give all customers 100% of your time and focus when serving them.

2. Develop a way to measure each standard. For example:

   a. We will answer the phone…(metric: question on customer survey)

   b. If someone is within 4 feet…(metric: random weekly observations per employee)

3. Regularly audit the standard to ensure that it is happening as planned. Remember, inspect what you expect and give your team feedback.

4. Ask a randomly selected group of loyal customers to inspect the standard and give you feedback. Of course, you should relay that feedback to your team as soon as possible.

2. Be Exceptional…Regardless of the Work Environment

Some people don't like where they work…at all. They may even despise who they report to. And since their work environment is so "toxic", they **choose** to withhold their best quality of work. "THIS PLACE does not deserve the best I have to offer. I will come to work, only do what is expected of me, collect my paycheck, and go home." Do you know anyone like that?

Bare Minimum

The problem with that line of thinking is that if you repeatedly choose to give the bare minimum, then eventually you will be comfortable giving the bare minimum. Yes, you would have unknowingly formed not only a habit, but a bad habit. At some point, you may not even know what excellent work looks like…and begin to think that you are not capable of being excellent. To be excellent is what you are called to be, and to be exceptional is what you are called to do.

> *"…if you repeatedly choose to give the bare minimum, then eventually you will be comfortable giving the bare minimum."*

Hot Tea

During a recent hotel stay, I decided that I wanted to have some hot tea late one night. Since it was a limited service hotel, ordering room service was not an option. It was around 11PM, and I called the front desk to see where I could possibly get some tea from. The employee told me, "Our restaurant has already closed, so tea will be available in the morning for breakfast". Click.

Now, I obviously knew that tea and hot water had to be available somewhere on the property, but I decided to wait and speak to the manager in the morning. When I spoke with the manager the next morning, he was upset about what happened and even showed me the employee mini-break area that was only a few feet behind the front desk. The break area had a refrigerator, and the refrigerator was stacked with…wait for it…tea! All types of tea.

So, here are a few reasons why the front desk agent may have responded the way he did:

a) He legitimately didn't know there was tea available (yeah right).

b) He is only comfortable working within the strict parameters of his job.

c) He doesn't like his job and/or where he works and has **chosen** not to do one more ounce than he absolutely has to.

Your Zeal

You cannot allow *anyone (or any work environment)* to rob you of your zeal to be exceptional. As difficult as it may be, you must push through any disdain you may have and honor your role, honor who you are serving and honor yourself. At some point, each person has to make a decision about how exceptional he/she wants to be, regardless of the work environment. Eventually, it can be quite fatiguing to constantly strive for excellence in a work environment that you can't stand to be in.

> *"You cannot allow anyone (or any work environment) to rob you of your zeal to be exceptional."*

In that case, see if you can address your discontentment with the appropriate people, or find somewhere else to work. But don't just find "any place" to work. Search for a company that has values which mirror your own. Ultimately, it's important to work for a company that you believe in.

Adjusting Your Service

Some people have a habit of adjusting their service based on how important they believe a particular customer is. One of the reasons that is so dangerous is because you really never know who you are serving or what their circumstances may be.

We have **no right** to treat anyone like they are "just a customer". That is simply wrong, and even immoral. Every customer has a story and it is our obligation to honor that customer regardless of what the story may be.

Never again be lulled into the fallacy that it's ok to give the bare minimum. Savagely fight that fallacy with everything you've got. Be exceptional despite the work environment. Stephen Covey wisely wrote, "Be an island of excellence in a sea of mediocrity". While that certainly can happen, try to find a team, manager and company that allow you to work among many islands of excellence in an ocean happy to have you there.

In the end, service has a purpose, and a noble purpose at that. We serve because serving is a good thing, and good things are worthy to be exalted. There is significance to your role. There is purpose to your role. If you truly understand what that means, then you have the ability to impact lives, one customer at a time.

Activity – Be Exceptional...Regardless of the Work Environment

Take the time to reflect on your job tasks. Make a list of the top 10 positive points. For each point indicate what you enjoy about it and one thing you can do to be exceptional at it.

Job Task	What I like about it	What I can do to be exceptional at it
1.		
2.		
3.		
4.		
5.		
6.		
7.		
8.		
9.		
10.		

3. Be Welcoming

As a follow up to my chapter about being eager to serve, it is important to highlight the importance of the entire welcome experience. There is a popular saying that goes, "You never get a second chance to make a first impression". While it is possible, it can be difficult to bounce back from a poor welcome experience.

Importance of the Welcome

On a recent trip, I drove up to the hotel where I would be staying. After receiving instructions from the doorman on where to go for self-parking, I made my way to the hotel and was immediately struck by how well-designed everything was. There were glass sculptures and beautiful chandeliers throughout the lobby. I was impressed. When I got to the front desk, there were two receptionists talking with each other. One of them eventually stopped talking, looked down at her computer, sighed, then said, "Hello, may I help you?" That question was asked with no eye contact, no smile, and no interest. That experience was the exact opposite of a warm welcome. The agent rushed through a scripted series of questions (Name? ID? Credit card?). It was abundantly clear that she either:

> "Whenever a customer enters your building, everyone must do all they can to create a welcoming atmosphere."

a)   Disliked her job.

b)   Disliked guests

c)   Was having a bad day

d)   Perhaps all of the above

Whatever the reason, I was very disappointed and felt unwelcome. That was clearly a wasted opportunity to make a great first impression and set my expectations for what the rest of the service could potentially be like. Whenever a customer enters your building, everyone must do all they can to create a welcoming atmosphere.

Imagine you haven't seen a favorite relative or a close friend for several years, and they come to visit. How will you greet them? More importantly, how will you make them feel? When a customer enters your building or walks up to your desk, they are entering your home.

Let's contrast that experience with a recent visit to the Relache Spa at the Gaylord Opryland Resort in Nashville, TN. As I entered through the spa's front door, I was immediately greeted by a receptionist with a big, warm smile...before I even got to the registration desk where she was. After welcoming me, she asked if I had a spa appointment. When I told her that I did, she quickly (yet gracefully) glanced at her appointment log, then proactively used my name to give me a more customized welcome. She then gave me an overview of the spa service that I reserved, along with a mini verbal orientation of the spa facilities.

That spa receptionist clearly:

- Loved her job

- Loved her guests

- Was having a great day (probably because she was in a job where she could fully use her talents for making others feel welcomed).

Needless to say, the rest of my spa experience, was on par with the warm greeting I received.

The Receptionist/Greeter

Many organizations severely undervalue the importance of the receptionist/greeter. That position is, by far, one of the most important in any service-driven business, regardless of the industry. That person can turn your bad day into a good one, or your good day into a bad one. Yes, that is how much power their smile (or frown) can have on the customer's experience. No one wants to walk into a restaurant and the hostess looks like she's been sucking on a lemon.

The receptionist, or whomever the first person is that your customer sees, should have the most natural smile on the entire team. They should love people and love making them feel welcome. They should come from behind their desk and periodically check on their guests. They should work the reception area/lobby, by straightening furniture, magazines, etc. They should be people filled with joy. Not necessarily people who are happy, because happiness is based on happenings. If the happenings are good, they are happy, and if the happenings are bad, they are unhappy. Joy is innate and grounded. Joyful people are appreciative. They appreciate that they have a job in the first place and they appreciate the opportunity to positively influence their customers.

So, here are my recommendations to design or re-design your welcome experience.

- Commit to <u>only hiring truly joyful people who can't help but to smile</u>. These types of people literally have to try NOT to smile because smiling is such a part of who they are.

- Work with your team to clearly articulate how you want your customers to feel every day for every guest.

- <u>Identify the key service touchpoints</u> in the welcome experience of your business (i.e. the parking lot, front door, reception desk, etc.)

- <u>Make deposits at those touchpoints</u> and look for opportunities to enhance them.

At the welcome experience, every customer should feel honored, as if they were the guest-of-honor at a banquet. So greet, smile and engage your customers from the moment that you see them. Not because you have to, but because it truly is your pleasure to do so.

ACTIVITY: Be Welcoming

1. List three things you will commit to doing this week to ensure you are providing a warm welcome to every customer, every time.

_____

_____

_____

_____

_____

2. List five non-verbal behaviors to avoid in order to make sure your customers feel welcome.

_____

_____

_____

_____

_____

_____

3. What are some words/phrases you can use to create a welcoming atmosphere?

    _____

    _____

    _____

    _____

    _____

    _____

4. If you are a supervisor, observe the way your team members are greeting their customers. Provide specific feedback about what is going well and what can be improved, to each team member.

4. Earn Your Customers' Confidence and Reap the Rewards

In any personal relationship, building trust is a key ingredient. Without trust, there really is no opportunity to deepen the relationship or have it evolve beyond the superficial stage. The same is true for customer relationships. To build trust and, loyalty with your customers, three elements are needed: competency, integrity, and follow through. Basically, if you know what you are doing, keep your promises, and follow through to ensure that your customers are happy, they will trust you. Even more, they will be confident in your ability to deliver an exceptional service experience every time. Earn your customer's confidence, reap the rewards.

Be Competent

Recently, I was invited to attend a gourmet food show, which featured a large exposition hall. Approximately one week before attending, I decided to call the customer service line to ask a few

"There is no substitute for being competent."

questions. First, I asked the customer service representative, "What time will the doors open?" She didn't know. Then I asked, "Will anything be on sale?" She didn't know that either. Finally, I asked approximately how many exhibitors will be in the expo hall. Her reply, "Sir, I don't know. I only work in a cubicle in the customer service department."

There is no substitute for being competent. If you don't know the answer to a question, then find out. If your goal is to build a culture of service excellence, then, "I don't know" is never acceptable

Have Integrity

It is commonly understood that you should do whatever you say you will do. Unfortunately, it is becoming increasingly common for people to do the exact opposite. Recently, an auto body technician assessed my car's damaged bumper and he promised to send an estimate to me by the following morning. I eventually got the estimate…over three days later. Have integrity. Think about how often businesses say they will call you, email you, or update you, and it never happens. Indeed, it is noticeable (and even admirable) when someone says they will do something and actually does it.

I recently had a question for the company that hosts my company's online store. I spoke with Kaci, who did not know the answer to my question, but she told me that she would find out and get back to me by the close of the business day. Kaci did exactly what she promised, and I am confident that if I have a question, that Kaci or someone on her team can assist.

Always Follow-Through

I have written previously about the importance of problem resolution and follow-through. The follow-through aspect is so important that it is worth revisiting. In my article, the 100% principle, I noted that whenever you receive a complaint, that you should follow up until you are certain that the customer is 100% satisfied with the resolution. We often times receive a complaint or request, initiate a resolution, then assume that everything will magically fall into place, culminating in a happy customer. Unfortunately, it rarely works out that way.

My team recently re-ordered a supply of our popular commitment cards that are sold on our website. Unfortunately, there was a printing error that made the cards unfit to be sold. So after we informed the vendor of the error, they apologized, re-printed the order and shipped it to us again. Now, here is the problem. No one from the vendor's office called or emailed us to follow-up and see if the new order was, in fact, printed to our satisfaction. Fortunately, it was…but what if it wasn't? The customer should never have to follow-up with you first.

"Being competent, having integrity, and following through are essential to building a relationship and earning your customers' confidence."

I realize the key points in this article can be deemed as *common sense*. If they are common sense, then why aren't they commonly done? Being competent, having integrity, and following through are essential to building a relationship and earning your customer's confidence. Continuously assess yourself, and assess your team to note where your strengths and opportunities for improvement are. If your customer's are confident in your ability to serve them, they will use your service more often and refer others to you as well. Perhaps, in the world of service, one of the most powerful phrases a customer can tell you is, I trust you and know that you will take care of me, regardless of the circumstance." Earn your customer's confidence and reap the rewards.

ACTIVITY: Earn Your Customers Confidence and Reap Rewards

1. **Be Competent** -Assess your own role, and take note of everything you ought to know. Identify the top 3 things that you need to learn more about and commit to a date that you will accomplish this.

_____

_____

_____

_____

_____

2. **Have Integrity** -Do not overpromise and under-deliver. Commit to under-promising and over delivering. Make a list of 3 questions you can ask your customers from time to time in order to gather feedback on how you are doing.

_____

_____

_____

_____

_____

3. **Always Follow Through** – Practice using the steps below and then make note of how the customer responded. Consider doing a role-play. For the service problem, use a common issue.

- Say you will own the complaint/request.

- Get the customer's contact information.

- Get the customer's preferred mode of contact (email, text, phone call).

- Begin the process of fixing the issue. Ensure that the resolution matches the complaint / request.

- If you need to pass the issue to another person/department, then do so. (But remember, that YOU still own it!).

- Proactively inform the customer on the status every 24 hours using the customer's preferred mode of contact.

- When you've received confirmation that the issue has been resolved, then contact the customer to inform them.

- Follow-up to ensure that the customer is, in fact, happy with the resolution.

_____

_____

_____

_____

_____

_____

5. Find a Way to Make It Happen

"...the most dedicated professionals, regardless of the request or the industry, find a way to make it happen."

"As long as it is legal, ethical, and moral, find a way to make it happen". That was the directive which was programmed into my brain very early in my career. I remember it vividly. It was on my first day of work at new employee orientation at the Ritz-Carlton, St. Thomas in 1996. The general manager passionately spoke about the need "to move heaven and earth to delight" our guests and creating memorable experiences every day. Although I worked in a luxury property before, it was obvious that this was another level of service excellence altogether. I love exceptional service, and I love people who are passionate about giving exceptional service. No matter where I've traveled, it is obvious that the most dedicated professionals, regardless of the request or the industry, find a way to make it happen.

Breakfast Buffet

On a recent trip to Jamaica, I was having dinner and asked the server if Ackee & Saltfish (Jamaican culinary staple) would be on the breakfast buffet the following morning.

Legal? = Yes   Ethical? = Yes   Moral? = Yes

The server told me that Ackee & Saltfish is only featured on the Sunday breakfast buffet; however, she will ensure that it would be available for me the following morning. Sure enough, when I went to breakfast, the hostess greeted me by name, then introduced me to my assigned server, who told me that the dish would be served to me shortly. Find a way to make it happen.

Pepperoni Pizza

Years ago, when I was a hotel concierge, a guest asked if it would be possible to get a Pizza Hut pepperoni pizza for dinner that evening.

Legal? = Yes   Ethical? = Yes   Moral? = Yes

Unfortunately, the closest Pizza Hut was 20 minutes away, and scheduled to close at 9PM that evening. It was now 8:45PM! I immediately called Pizza Hut to see if they would be willing to make the pizza and I would personally pick it up. They said "Yes", and I was able to pick up the pizza and have it delivered to the guest's room. Find a way to make it happen.

One Customer

Some people view the number "1" as an insignificant number. One of anything is not enough. In the business sense, having "only" one customer might be considered dismal. On the contrary, by learning how to cherish that one customer, you will learn how to attract and retain many more.

By not slowing down, appreciating and being thankful for one, we miss the true beauty of how fortunate we actually are. Sometimes having no customers is the best medicine to re-focus on how important one customer is. Honor that one customer…give thanks for that one customer…promise yourself to never take that one customer for granted ever again. Find a way to keep that one customer happy and engaged.

In the case of service excellence, imagine if you and your team only had one customer to serve for the next week. (Financially, your team has enough money so the business is not in danger of shutting down). How would your team cherish that one customer? I would imagine that you would:

- Be grateful for that customer's patronage (and tell him/her so)
- Have a sense of urgency and be eager to serve
- Learn that customer's preferences, then act on them
- Not only comply, but anticipate that customer's needs
- Understand that even though you have a lot of service and attentiveness to give, that, ultimately, service is about what THAT customer wants (which, in some cases, may be to leave him/her alone)

I firmly believe that by truly understanding the importance of honoring "one" customer, then the patronage of many will soon follow.

> *"Take it as your personal mission to find a way...any way...to make it happen for every customer."*

In truth, it doesn't really matter what the request is, or the industry, or the time of day. As long as the request is legal, ethical and moral, begin by assuming that you can, in fact, make it happen. Just make it happen. Find a way. That is the true beauty and splendor of service excellence. That is what transforms the simple touchpoint into one with heart and soul. Value, cherish and honor that touchpoint. Take it as your personal mission to find a way...any way...to make it happen for every customer.

As long as it is legal, ethical, and moral:

- ...never say "no"
- ...suggest alternative options
- ...assume that you can accommodate the request

By consistently doing so, you will notice an increased vitality in your work (and life). No request or complaint will seem insurmountable. You may actually begin to look forward to requests, just to see how you can challenge yourself to make it happen. In the end, the ultimate benefactor will be the customer, and THAT, above all else, is why we find a way.

ACTIVITY: Find a Way to Make it Happen

For each listed action, think of ways to make it even more consistent and effective on your team.

Actions	Notes
Be grateful for that customer's patronage (and tell him/her so)	
Have a sense of urgency and be eager to serve	
Learn that customer's preferences, then act on them	
Not only comply, but anticipate that customer's needs	
Service is about what THAT customer wants (which, in some cases, may be to leave him/her alone)	

6. Four Lessons All Businesses Can Learn from a 5-Star Resort

Have you ever experienced service so pure that you could literally feel it? Service that is unpretentious, unrestrictive, unscripted, yet seamless and professional all at the same time. Even as a service consultant, it would have been difficult for me to imagine that such a caliber of service could exist so flawlessly and naturally. I am referring to a recent memorable experience during a trip to the Ayana Resort & Spa in Bali. I wish that I could pack up a few of the staff and take them around the world with me so they can show everyone what excellence, humility and professionalism look like. Everything from the shuttle driver offering chilled face cloths, to a framed photo (of my family) in the villa, the attention-to-detail was inspiring. Here are four quick lessons that anyone, in any industry, can learn from them.

Expect Perfection

There is no question in my mind that the staff at Ayana is very proud of their property and the service that they provide. Since the team has so much pride in what they do, it makes sense that, for them, good is never good enough. Even if 99 out of 100 guests have a stellar service experience, the staff will listen, empathize, fix, and follow-up to ensure that the disappointed guest is happy from that moment on. Striving to be perfect is not a disappointing activity (that some cynical observers may label as "pointless"). On the contrary, there is an obvious difference in how diligently one prepares, when the goal is to score 100%. Think about students who are studying for a test. Those students who have made up their mind to get every question correct actually score 100% more often than students who study *just to pass*. In fact, students who study for, and expect to receive a 100% are actually quite disappointed (even shocked), if they receive anything less.

Takeaway: Develop the habit of preparing for and expecting a 100% flawless service experience every day, for every customer, at every touchpoint. You and your team might be astonished at the results.

Be Thankful

> *"I believe that there is a strong linkage between being thankful and delivering great service."*

To understand the Ayana Resort & Spa's service quality, it is important to appreciate the "thankful" nature of the Balinese culture. Balinese people are used to giving thanks multiple times per day for such things as food, shelter, health, and life. Most people I know take those things for granted and have a sense of entitlement, as if such things are owed to them. I believe that there is a strong linkage between being thankful and delivering great service. I am not inferring that being thankful is the ultimate panacea to cure the world's customer service woes, but I do see a strong relationship between the two.

Start your day (everyday) by being genuinely thankful for life, food, shelter, and clothing. Being thankful and appreciative removes the entitlement factor that can dilute the ability to genuinely be of service to others. Entitlement is a selfish characteristic because the focus is on yourself. It is difficult to be focused on yourself *AND* give engaging service to others at the same time. So, regularly ask yourself, "What am I thankful for?" and "What would life be like if I did not have those things?

> **Takeaway: Always be appreciative of the opportunity to be of service and to positively impact someone else's day (or life).*

Connect the Touchpoints…Seamlessly

As you will recall from my earlier articles, a touchpoint is any interaction between the customer and the business. The Ayana team did an amazing job of connecting the touchpoints so there was never a moment where I felt lost or not taken care of. For example, allow me to share my spa experience at the resort.

- As I approached the front desk, the staff was smiling, as if they had been waiting all day just to see me (keep in mind that the resort was 98% full at the time).
- I was warmly greeted, then was escorted to the spa's open-air welcome lounge, where I was offered a seat and a delicious "welcome" drink (a cold hibiscus beverage).

- Shortly thereafter, another attendant brought me a short form to complete (standard spa questionnaire that covers health concerns, past spa visits, allergies, etc.).

- Next, I was taken to the locker room entrance, where another attendant eagerly awaited. He directed me to my assigned locker, explained the locker operation and asked me to change into my spa gear (robe, slippers).

- I was then escorted out of the locker room to meet the massage therapist, who was smiling of course (seriously… I have never seen so many happy and smiling people in the same place at the same time).

- As the therapist brought me to the massage room, he confirmed which massage I was scheduled for and then gave me an articulate overview of that massage's health benefits.

- The rest of the spa experience flowed along the same lines.

Takeaway: Map out the customer experience from start to finish, per department.

Kaizen

Kaizen is a Japanese term that means "improvement". In the business sense, it is often referred to as having *continuous, incremental improvement over time.* Essentially, next month you should be better than you were this month, and next year you should be better than you were this year. In 2010, Ayana Resort's spa (Thermes Marins Spa) was voted as the #1 spa in the world by Conde Nast Traveller Magazine. Their staff is amazing. In all of my travels, their spa team is second to none; yet, they are

> *"…I have found that the people and organizations that are the most eager to improve, are the ones who are currently the best."*

constantly looking for ways to improve. Many people and organizations believe that once you've reached a certain level, then there is no longer a need to aggressively learn or seek improvement opportunities. Interestingly, I have found that the people and organizations that are the most eager to improve, are the ones who are *currently* the best. Olympic gold medalists often train harder to win additional gold medals in future Olympics. They believe that anyone can be world-class on any given day. Almost like a fluke. However, it takes dedication, passion, and a strong vision for excellence to create consistent world-class performance.

Takeaway: Excellence is not a destination, but an ongoing journey.

Be bold enough to expect perfection, be thankful, connect the touchpoints, and strive for continuous improvement on a daily basis. Don't try to keep up with the competition, but rather strive to become the benchmark in everything you do. Encourage your team to dream…and dream big. As you assess your team's current service acumen, it is important to appreciate where you are, but imagine where you could be.

ACTIVITY: Four Lessons All Businesses Can Learn From a Five Star Resort

For each lesson, identify what you can do to put it into action on your team.

Lessons	
1. Expect Perfection	*Develop the habit of preparing for and expecting a 100% flawless service experience every day, for every customer, at every touchpoint.*
What will you do to apply this to your job?	
2. Be Thankful	*Always be appreciative of the opportunity to be of service and to positively impact someone else's day (or life).*
What will you do to apply this to your job?	
3. Connect the Touchpoints...Seamlessly	*Map out the customer experience from start to finish.*
What will you do to apply this to your job?	

4. Continuously Improve (Kaizen)	*Excellence is not a destination, but an ongoing journey.*

What will you do to apply this to your job?

7. Give What You Can With What You Have

> *"Anyone, in any setting, in any industry CAN provide a memorable service experience (if they really want to)."*

There is so much to be said for attentiveness, warmth, and competency. Those three elements have the potential to turn any experience into a 5-star event. As I've noted previously, a 5-star experience is not necessarily about having luxurious surroundings. I have experienced world-class service in some of the most unlikely places. That, to me, is the most inspiring part of all. Anyone, in any setting, in any industry CAN provide a memorable service experience (if they really want to).

The Grand Bazaar

During a trip to Istanbul, Turkey I had an opportunity to visit the famous Grand Bazaar. The Grand Bazaar is one of the largest and oldest covered markets in the world. It contains over 3000 small shops, and some of the shops are so small that it's hard to turn around without bumping into something. One clothing store that I entered was similarly small. The store owner gave me a warm welcome, invited me to have a seat (on a box), and offered a complimentary cup of green tea. We had not even discussed me buying clothes yet! I ended up purchasing a leather jacket and a few other items. *Give what you can...with what you have.*

Gypsy Taxi

Something major happened to me when I was still living on St. Thomas, and it helped shape my entire outlook on service. I was a junior in high school, and ended up missing the 6:30AM school bus. Fortunately, I had a few dollars with me, so I walked a few miles to a nearby shopping center, where I knew that "gypsy" taxis would be. Years ago in St. Thomas, we referred to gypsy taxis as any cab that didn't belong to an official taxi company; basically, anyone with a car who wanted to make a little extra money could be a gypsy taxi. As I approached the shopping center, there was only one driver available. We walked to his car, and I noticed that it looked broken down, with peeling paint. Plus, a headlight was loosened. Then something remarkable happened.

He opened the car door for me (back seat), had a newspaper on the backseat and was very polished (yet warm) in his conversation with me as we drove. He even referred to me as, "Mr. Bryan". Keep in mind that I was 16 years old at the time. I am now in my mid-thirties and have been chauffeured many times in towncars and other luxury vehicles around the globe. With a few exceptions over the years, I have not come across anyone who is on the caliber of that gypsy taxi driver. Some of the most memorable service is what you deliver from your heart, regardless of the resources you have.

Gratitude

Ultimately, providing great service is a conscious decision. It's not something that can or should be begrudgingly done. Genuinely engaging service should be heartfelt. It should make the customer feel like you are interested in his/her well-being. No matter how brief the service experience is, customers should feel like their well-being is important to whoever is serving them.

> *"One thing I have noticed that separates some of the best service from the rest is gratitude."*

So, how can this all be translated into action steps? We can go through the usual list that contains things like "smile, anticipate needs, follow-up on customer complaints, etc., etc.". Truthfully, a quick Google search can reveal a similar list. Even attentiveness, warmth and competency are fairly common action items. One thing that I've noticed that separates some of the best service from the rest is *gratitude*. Often times, the best service comes from people who exude a strong sense of gratitude. These are appreciative for not only having a job, but also are happy for the opportunity to serve others. It's unmistakable. There seems to be an inner-joy that may or not be reflective of their socio-economic place in the world. But the joy that they infuse into their service makes them seem abundantly wealthy. You almost look at them in awe. Even more beautiful, is how they manage to make EVERY customer feel like he/she is the only one being served at the moment.

One of the best things you can do is to acknowledge and celebrate those service superstars when you see them. Chances are that they don't nearly the type of recognition that you might expect. If the world had more taxi drivers and

Bazaar shop owners like I described, I can't help but think that the overall level of service worldwide would improve as well.

ACTIVITY: Give What You Can With What You Have

Practice with a partner. Pick a co-worker to be your partner. Share this with them and then commit to doing something unexpected for your customers. Only use whatever resources you already have available to you. Discuss what you did and how the customer reacted.

Partners Name:	
Set the Goal:	
What was the Customers Reaction:	

8. Honor Your Customers

The more I think about it, the more I realize that serving is about honoring. Hoteliers and spa professionals honor their guests...healthcare professionals honor their patients...educators honor their students and so on. To fully understand what this article is about, let us first define "honor". A quick review of any dictionary will find that the word, honor, means to show high respect or to hold in high esteem. No matter the specific term used, each of your customers deserves to feel honored, regardless of who they are or whether they have been classified as a VIP or not.

Be Present

"Every customer should get the best version of us at any given time..."

When our computers freeze up, many of us press "Ctrl-Alt-Delete" to refresh the screen and start over. Wouldn't it be great if we all had Ctrl-Alt-Delete buttons on our bodies to "refresh" ourselves before serving each customer? Every customer should get the best version of us at any given time, but, truthfully, that can become difficult if you are serving dozens or even hundreds of customers per day.

I recently came across a blog post by **The Domestic Life Stylist**. In it, the author wrote,

"Commit to yourself that whatever type of day you have, you will commit yourself first to be present. Be present in your mind, in your space and in your spirit. Be present in your thought as you spend time with your kids, be present if you only have 15 minutes to exercise, be present even if you only have 5 minutes to yourself in the shower."

Half attention just will not cut it. Either give your full attention to what you are doing or nothing at all.

Honor People

If service is about honoring others, then the assumption is that people, in general, are worthy of being valued. During my last physical check-up, the physician took to the time to explain the purpose and steps of the next procedure before he actually did it. He explained the purpose of looking into my eyes, testing my reflexes and listening to my lungs. As a patient, I felt incredibly valued that he took the time to be so thorough.

Whenever you take the time to tell your customers about the service they will receive, they feel honored, appreciated and valued. Essentially, the message is that if I value you, I will keep you informed.

ACTIVITY: Honor Your Customers

What are you going to do differently every day, starting today, to honor your customers? Make a decision of what that is, make sure you do it every day. Make your plan for the next ten days.

Day	Today I will...	How did it go?
1		
2		
3		
4		
5		
6		
7		
8		
9		
10		

9. How to Serve a VIP

> *"...serving the Queen of England is just as honorable as serving Joe Smith, who is on vacation with his family of four."*

When I was a line employee in the hotel business, I would usually be the person assigned to serve the VIP guests. Whether I was a server or a concierge, my managers trusted me to provide exceptional customer service to the CEO's, celebrities, and royalty that would visit. In my manager's minds, those guests needed "extra special service". While I was flattered that my managers thought so highly of my customer service skills, I was always bothered by their assertion that some guests should get "better" treatment than others should. In my mind, **all** of my guests were VIP's. I truly never made a distinction between how I served the supposed VIP's and every other guest I had. In my heart, I felt (and still feel) that EVERYONE deserves excellent service, regardless of their socioeconomic status, job title, or any other label. For me, serving the Queen of England is just as honorable as serving Joe Smith, who is on vacation with his family of four.

First Class vs. Coach

As many of you know, I am a frequent traveler and one of the perks of travelling often is being upgraded to the first-class cabin. While I enjoy the larger seats and additional amenities, there is one thing that bothers me: I am often treated much nicer by the flight attendants in first-class, than when I am in coach. It's like a completely different service experience, although I'm on the same plane.

A company that is truly striving to build a "world-class" service culture will make every effort to develop service standards that emphasize exceptional service for EVERY customer, all the time. Now, this does not mean that every customer should get the same service. True service excellence requires personalization and making each customer feel as though there is no one else, at that moment, more important than him or her. Using customer's names and learning their preferences are two ways to accomplish personalized service.

Service is NOT about what you want to give

I have witnessed many occasions when someone tried to be engaging, but ended up annoying and disengaging the customer. For example, wrestling a suitcase from a guest who would rather carry it herself is annoying. Insisting on

"...service is not about what you want to give, it is about what the other person wants to receive."

escorting a customer, when he has already declined your offer is annoying. Trying to establish an engaging dialogue, when it's clear that the customer would rather be left alone is annoying. As I have written previously, service is not about what you want to give, it is about what the other person wants to receive.

Give "insider" tips

One of the best ways to make your customers feel like a VIP is by giving them insider information. In other words, making your customers feel like they are privy to valuable information that is not widely known (or at least they may perceive that the information is not widely known). For example, Enterprise Rent-a-Car has a service called, **We'll pick you up**. This basically means that the Enterprise location, where you are renting the car, can send a shuttle to pick you up from wherever you are (home, office, etc.) and bring you back to their branch to rent the car. I recently saw an employee tell a customer about that service and the customer was incredibly impressed. The customer commented that he thought that such service was only reserved for their big-shot clients.

At a recent trip to the CVS Pharmacy in our neighborhood, an employee saw a shopper looking at canned salmon (yes, CVS sells grocery items too). The employee proactively approached the shopper and told him that the salmon was half price, even though the displayed price did not reflect the reduced price. The employee explained that every week, the CVS sales paper contains deals that only those who subscribe to receive the sales paper, will know about. How do you think that shopper felt? You guessed it, like a VIP.

So, here are a few simple tips on how to serve everyone like a VIP:

- Have a sense of urgency for everyone, regardless of their "status".

- Tell yourself, "this is the most important person I will serve today".

- Remind yourself that every customer has at least one preference. Challenge yourself to identify it, act on it, and share it with your team.

Everyone deserves to receive world-class service. Whether they are in a gas station, hospital, spa, hotel, bank, taxi, or airplane, excellent service is excellent service. Your customers will appreciate your eagerness to serve and reward you with their patronage, their referrals, and their loyalty.

ACTIVITY: How to Serve a VIP

What are examples of "insider information" that you can offer your customers?

_____

_____

_____

_____

_____

_____

_____

_____

_____

_____

_____

_____

_____

_____

10. Lead Me

Every day there are many employees who go to work, and are looking for one thing. No, the one thing I am referring to has nothing to do with compensation. The "one thing" is more intrinsic in nature. These employees are looking to be *inspired.* Tony Zseigh, CEO of

> *"...being inspired resonates on a much deeper level and tends to last longer than being merely motivated, which may not be as enduring."*

Zappos.com, made a very interesting statement that really resonated with me. He said, "At Zappos.com, we stopped looking for ways to motivate our team and started looking for ways to inspire them." The connotation is that being inspired resonates on a much deeper level and tends to last longer than being merely motivated, which may not be as enduring.

On a personal note, I know that my greatest contributions at work almost always happened after I felt inspired to do more than what was expected. I've been fortunate to have had multiple mentors throughout my career. These mentors guided me, challenged me, and yes, inspired me to see more, do more and become more. The purpose of this article is to shed some light on what it takes to inspire your team to become more than they realize they can be.

So, here are six things that inspire people at work (from the employee's perspective):

1. **A compelling vision:** Much has been written about vision statements. Truly, the vision is the primary tool that great leaders use to influence (not mandate) others to follow them. The vision should clearly explain where the leader expects the team to be years from now.

   * Voice of the Employee: *"I want to be on a winning team. I need to know where we are going. Please tell me. After all, if I know where we are going, I will be more inclined to help us get there. Lead Me."*

2. **Clearly articulated mission:** The mission should easily show what your team does, how your team does it, why it does it, and who it does it for. The central purpose of why your team exists should be readily found in the mission.

> *** Voice of the Employee:** "I want to be clear about what we do. Even more than that, I want to be proud of what we do. I want to brag to my family and friends about the great team I am on. Lead me."*

3. **Alignment between the vision and mission:** One of the biggest gaps many companies have is that there is no clear connection between where the company is going (vision), what the company does (mission) and individual employee job performance. When employees can see how their specific job contributes to the organization's success, they are more likely to put more effort into their work.

> *** Voice of the Employee:** "I need to know how I fit into the bigger picture. Is my specific job even that important? The vision and mission both sound good, but I don't know how I can possibly help fulfill them. Lead me."*

4. **Connect to a greater purpose** (*Special Note.. This point is especially relevant for Generation Y and Millennials*): Even beyond your company's vision and mission, why is your company's existence a benefit to society. Why is the world any better because your company is in it?

> *** Voice of the Employee:** "I need to know how this company contributes to the well-being of society. How does the service and/or product we provide help to improve people's lives? Are we volunteering our time, donating to charities and being environmentally responsible? Lead me."*

5. **Learn both personal and professional goals:** Beyond the daily work that your staff does, take the time to learn each of your employees' professional and personal goals. As the old saying goes, people buy into the leader before they buy into the leadership.

> *** Voice of the Employee:** "I need you to know me, and understand me. Take the time to learn both my professional and personal goals. Challenge me to achieve them. Mentor me, coach me, and follow-up with me. Lead me."*

6. **Uncompromising leadership:** One of the fastest ways to de-motivate your best staff is they see you accepting mediocrity from the rest of the team. Do NOT compromise your high expectations. If you do, one of

the first ramifications is a once-great employee will decide to either quit-and-leave OR quit-and-stay.

* Voice of the Employee: *"I need you to set high expectations and commit to them. Please don't compromise them. As easy as it is to look the other way when a team member doesn't pick up that piece of paper, please say something. I love my job and I love this company, but I don't want to be a part of a losing team. I want us to win. This team deserves to win and winning teams have winning leaders. These leaders do not tolerate foolishness. My only professional dream is to work for a team AND a leader who are both committed to excellence. Have I found them? Lead me."*

ACTIVITY: Lead Me

Practice inspiring people. If you supervise a team, you can work on inspiring your team members. If you don't, you can work on inspiring your peer group.

What inspires people.	How can you use this to inspire?
A compelling vision	
Clearly articulated mission	
Alignment between the vision and mission	
Connect to a greater purpose	
Learn both personal and professional goals	
Uncompromising leadership	

11. Lessons from a 5-Star/Diamond Restaurant

Years ago, I heard a French wine maker say, "Good is not good enough; in fact, it has to be perfect all the time". He was referring to the detail and care that goes into growing grapes at his winery. That one quote captures the essence of what a 5-star/5-diamond restaurant strives for. I recently dined at Lautrec, which is a 5-star/5-diamond restaurant at the Nemacolin Woodlands Resort in Farmington, PA. While I have dined in exceptional restaurants in the past, this was among the best in the world, by far. So, in the spirit of *Give.Share.Teach*, I would like to highlight some key points that anyone (in any industry) can learn from Lautrec.

Reverence

One of the first things customers should notice is that they are the absolute focus of your team's attention. At Lautrec, I felt like I was the guest of honor at a high-profile gala. The beautiful thing is that I am sure that every guest felt that way also. Being a 5-Star/5 diamond restaurant means that you have a laser-like focus on whomever you happen to be serving at the moment; whether it is for 15 seconds or 15 minutes.

Personal Touches

At Lautrec, the attention-to-detail is key. For example, my name was printed on the menu. Beyond looking "cool", the customized menu signified that they were prepared for me and cared enough to add a special touch. Again, every guest received this. You see, it's not enough to be exemplary every now and then. 5-star/5-diamond means that you are exemplary ALL the time. To a certain degree, you have to maintain a binary view of the products and services you offer. They should be either exceptional, or completely poor. When you are trying to deliver a world-class service experience, it can be dangerous to have gray areas. Those gray areas can easily multiply and infect other services and products that you are offering.

Knowledge

At Lautrec, my server literally knew everything about everything on the menu. When I asked him about champagne, he told me about the taste, the region the grapes were grown, the temperature and a little story about the

"True service professionals stand out from the crowd because of their commitment to excellence."

winemaker. When I asked about a salad item, he went into similar and exciting detail. The server spoke about garden greens like they were the greatest creation of mankind. He was not only very knowledgeable, but he was *happy* to be very knowledgeable. True service professionals stand out from the crowd because of their commitment to excellence.

Gracious Goodbye

At Lautrec, the farewell experience was just as memorable as the welcoming experience. I received a tour of the kitchen and the culinary staff was waiting to greet and thank me for coming in. At the end of the tour, the chef signed the menu, then rolled it up like a scroll as a memento.

"Good is not good enough; in fact, it has to be perfect all the time."

Not everyone is willing to work in an environment where excellence is expected every day. That statement is true for both leaders and line staff. As an employee, you have to bring a certain amount of innate passion, pride and professionalism to the job. As a leader, you must have an eye for detail, expect excellence every day, and maintain a healthy intolerance for mediocrity. But above all, a leader in a 5-star/5-diamond caliber team MUST model the service they expect to see.

Perhaps the biggest lesson I took from Lautrec is that there is something special and inspiring about caring deeply for your craft. That caring is manifested through reverence, personal touches and being knowledgeable, among other things. Good is not good enough; in fact, it has to be perfect all the time.

ACTIVITY: Lessons from a 5-Star/Diamond Restaurant

Discuss the following questions with your team (if you supervise a team), or with your peers.

1. What can you and your team do to make your customer's feel like they are the guest of honor at a banquet?

   _____

   _____

   _____

   _____

2. How can you and your team customize the experience more for each customer?

   _____

   _____

   _____

   _____

3. What information should everyone on your team know about their profession, company, and industry?

_____

_____

_____

_____

4. How can you and your team enhance the farewell experience?

_____

_____

_____

_____

12. Memorable. Valuable. Relevant.

At the end of the day, service is really about making someone feel cared for. That's it. We can talk about steps of service, touchpoints, and exceeding expectations until we are exhausted, but if your customers don't feel like you genuinely care about them (or their issue), then true service really has not taken place. To make that point clearer, I propose that for service to be special, it must be three things: Memorable. Valuable. Relevant. The customer should remember it, find it valuable, and be relevant to their specific issue.

The Birthday

A friend of mine was travelling on business to Minneapolis and stayed at the Sofitel Hotel. His birthday happened to be during this trip, and while his clients remembered and wished him, happy birthday, some of his family members back home didn't. Suffice to say, he was a bit depressed that evening. While at dinner, a server noticed his demeanor and inquired if he was OK. He decided to share his story, and she immediately wished him a happy birthday. Also, the server went and told all of her colleagues in the restaurant and throughout the hotel about his birthday. Several employees put some money together and went to the hotel gift store to buy a birthday card and everyone signed it. They presented the signed card to him before he finished dinner. Memorable. Valuable. Relevant.

Enterprise Rent-A-Car

On a trip to Denver, Colorado, I met a textbook example of someone who works like he owns it. He is a shuttle bus driver for the Enterprise Rent-a-car location at Denver International Airport. When I left the main airline terminal and walked outside to the Enterprise shuttle, he was eagerly waiting to greet the approaching passengers, and said, "Welcome to Denver!" One passenger had a baby and a baby stroller, so before beginning to drive, he reminded her to ensure that the stroller wheels were locked in place.

He then inquired if it was anyone's first trip to Denver. He followed up by announcing the weather forecast for that evening and the following day. When I say that he gave the weather forecast, I don't just mean the high and low temperatures. The driver went into full TV meteorologist-mode and gave the wind conditions, precipitation, chance of snow, etc. He then inquired if anyone was planning to go skiing while in town. One gentleman answered yes, and he then told him the phone # (and specific phone extension) for the "roadside conditions hotline". Memorable. Valuable. Relevant.

Give Anyway

Sometimes you will serve with all your heart, and not get a "thank you". Give anyway. Not only may they not thank you, but in the MIDST of you serving, they may complain about something else. Give anyway. As difficult as it may be sometimes, your genuine service to others should not be dependent upon whether they say thank you or not. Of course, we are all human and have feelings so a little appreciation would be nice. But do not make your service delivery contingent upon other people's gratitude. Give anyway.

> *"Sometimes you will serve with all your heart, and not get a 'thank you'. Give anyway."*

Culture

Often times, people ask me about the first thing they should do to develop a team of people who deliver engaging service. The first thing I tell them is to make service the most important thing on the team. It cannot be equal to any other objective, and it certainly can't be an item on a to-do list (i.e. Service will be a key focus this year). Every process on your team has to be anchored in service. Basically, anyone should be able to look at ANY of your team members, and see that exceptional service is how the team measures its success. Furthermore, any new employee should be able to immediately tell from the interview that "this team is different from any other team that I've been a part of".

> *"The immense power of a kind word, gesture or action can have lasting effects that transcend your company's mission."*

The immense power of a kind word, gesture or action can have lasting effects that transcend your company's mission. In order for customers to feel deeply cared for, your team has to deeply care about service. So go ahead and create memorable, valuable and relevant experiences for as many people as you can.

Your customers will appreciate it and you will create a competitive advantage that is hard to imitate, match or beat.

ACTIVITY: Memorable. Valuable. Relevant.

What is one thing that your customers will always remember about the services or products your team provides? (If nothing is apparent, then brainstorm something that is impactful that will stay in your customer's memory for years to come.)

_____

_____

_____

_____

_____

_____

13. Independent & Empowered: A Letter To My Manager

When I think of empowerment, one word comes to mind: Independent. To me, independence means to be free...without restrictions. As an employee, I need to know that you (my manager) trusts and believes in me enough to empower me to serve with excellence. No, I don't mean just having a clever mission statement that claims that the staff is empowered. Rather, do you encourage me to think independently to come up with a solution to a customer problem? Do you genuinely solicit my input and ideas, then challenge me to help implement those ideas? Do you empower me to recognize my peers (in my department and others)? Do you challenge me to go beyond merely meeting expectations, and seek ways to exceed them?

All of those things are key to fostering a culture of independence. Customers judge the quality of the service experience by the responsiveness of the first person they speak with to address their issue.

"Customers judge the quality of the service experience by the responsiveness of the first person they speak with to address their issue."

Trust me, I want to work like I own it, but I also need you, my manager, to treat me like I own it. Being exceptional is a deeply personal decision. No one can MAKE me work like I own it. Whenever people do things they don't like to do, it shows. However, since I have honor for what I do, I will consistently strive to do my work in the best possible light.

Chances are that I may never tell you to challenge me, but I need you to. Chances are that I may never tell you to recognize me for a job well done, but I need you to.

There is nothing quite like coming to work with the expectation that I can do whatever it takes to create memorable experiences for our customers. As long as it is legal, ethical and moral, I need the empowerment to find a way to make it happen.

Although I know that I am independent, I also know that I can't create a culture of service excellence on my own. I need my team mates and other departments. If we all share the same mindset, then every touchpoint will be exceptional for every customer every day.

Bonus:

In my opinion, independence and empowerment are hallmarks of luxury service. I recently came across an article by renowned concierge, James Ridenour, and he perfectly articulated what distinguishes excellent service from luxury service.

"The Oxford Dictionary defines service as 'The action of helping or doing work for someone'. For me, the definition of luxury service is most clearly defined in the way I train my team. I teach them that the difference between four-star hotel service (excellent service) and five-star service (luxury service) is that in a four-star hotel everything the guest asks for is provided in an efficient and courteous manner, whereas in a five start hotel the guest shouldn't even have to ask - their needs should be anticipated. The goal should be for the guest to be *surprised and delighted by a level of service that delivers not only on their expectations but actually exceeds them.*" - James Ridenour

ACTIVITY: Independent & Empowered: A Letter to My Manager

Write a letter to your Manager. Tell them how they currently trust, believe, and empower you to serve with excellence. Include things they can do better or differently if they don't trust, believe, or empower you. Also, include one thing that you do exceptionally well, and explain that the team may benefit from you doing it consistently.

_____

_____

_____

_____

_____

_____

_____

_____

_____

_____

_____

_____

14. It's About Your Heart

"If I have no other qualities, I can succeed with love alone. Without it, I will fail though I possess all the knowledge and skills of the world. I will greet each day with love in my heart."
—Og Mandino

It's about your heart. With all I've written about touchpoints, anticipating needs and steps of service, none of them can compare with your heart. Your heart is what connects with people. Your heart is what allows you to listen empathetically. Your heart is what causes you to give a genuine smile to a complete stranger, who you find yourself now serving. Yes, the heart is what pushes you to love. Love IS service, and service IS love. To create consistent, world-class service on your team, there must be a regular discussion about the heart and its role in driving service excellence.

> *"Love IS service, and service IS love."*

S.I.F.I. (Superficially interesting, but fundamentally insignificant)

There are those who will mentally fast-forward through any discussion (or article) about the heart. They view this topic as superficially interesting, but fundamentally insignificant. In their minds, they believe that tactics and strategy, alone, will enable them to accomplish their service objectives. Tactics and strategy are not bad things. In fact, they are a necessity. But tactics and strategy are incomplete without a discussion about the heart. Imagine a beautiful car with no driver, or a sleek jet with no pilot. Without the heart, tactics and strategy are simply shiny hunks of metal with no soul.

> *"They don't look at service excellence solely as a competitive advantage, but rather as their sacred duty."*

If you look at some of the world's most iconic service companies like Disney and Four Seasons, you will notice that they are blatantly open about their hearts and how much they care about who they serve. They don't look at service excellence solely as a competitive advantage, but rather as their sacred duty.

So, how do we make the heart our central focus in delivering great service?

1. Be thankful for the opportunity to serve people who actually want the service/product you provide. Not only do they want it, but they want it from YOU! Don't take that for granted.

2. Challenge yourself to WOW somebody every day.

3. Before asking for anything, offer to give something first. Remember: Give-Share-Teach.

4. Learn at least one preference about one customer every day (preferred name, hobby, pet peeves, favorite food/beverage, preferred mode of communication, line of work, birthday, anniversary date, favorite TV show, favorite music genre, etc.). The list can go on and on.

5. Tell your customers how much you appreciate them (and mean it!)

"But I'm too busy! There's no possible way I can make each customer feel taken care of." Do what you can with what you have. Regardless if you have 30 seconds or 30 minutes, approach each customer with kindness in your heart. Always ask yourself, "how can I do more than the bare minimum with this customer?" By asking that question of yourself every day, you will actually be forming a very powerful thing known as a habit. And since it is a good habit, allow it to take root and flourish.

More than the fancy furniture, expensive equipment, chandeliers, and manicured lawns, every customer is saying, "I want you to know me, pay attention to me, and care about me!" Love is service. Service is love. Use your heart to reach other hearts and success will surely follow.

ACTIVITY: It's About Your Heart

What do you commit to doing for your customers that is more than the "bare minimum"? More than what is expected?

_____

_____

_____

_____

_____

_____

_____

_____

_____

_____

15. My Job Is Nothing Without You

"If it weren't for these customers, I could get my job done!" Believe it or not, I have heard that exact phrase on more than one occasion. Some people view the customer as an interruption of their work. In their minds, customer's complicate things, cause stress, and get in the way of an, otherwise, enjoyable job. The point that is sorely missing is…THERE IS NO JOB without customers. It may sound ridiculously obvious, but many people completely miss that point. Customers are not an interruption of your work, they are the purpose of it.

> *"You are either serving the customer, or you are serving someone who is."*

In my mind, serving, giving, sharing, helping and teaching are all pointing to the exact same thing. *Regardless of the industry, everyone's job exists to do something for someone else.* Period. You are either serving the customer, or you are serving someone who is.

Honor

Being exceptional is a deeply personal decision. No one can MAKE you work like you own it. Whenever people do things they don't like to do, it shows. However, if there is honor for what you do, then you will consistently strive to present your work in the best possible light.

Busy

Does this sound familiar? "If the lines weren't so long…if I didn't have so many emails…if I didn't have so many requests, **then** I could get my job done." Never complain when you are busy. Rather, be happy and grateful when you are busy. Be appreciative that anyone wants your product or service in the first place. That is what gives your role its significance; it's reason to exist.

The Last Person

The last person you serve at the end of your shift, should not feel like they are the last person being served at the end of your shift.

If I was coming to your house for Thanksgiving dinner, and arrived late, I'm sure that you would still be hospitable (offer to fix me a plate, etc.). Similarly, if

I come to your breakfast buffet five minutes before closing, I should not see you hurrying…rushing to break down the buffet. That would make me feel unwelcomed. In fact, the message is, "We've got things to do, and you (the customer) are getting in the way".

I will

Since I know that the customer is not an interruption of my job, but rather the purpose of it, how will I behave?

I will begin each day with immense gratitude that I have, yet, another opportunity to earn a living.

I will abandon any sense of job entitlement, and always strive to re-earn the right to have this job, every day.

I will do my job in such a way that guarantees my customers will return whenever the opportunity arises.

I will honor the fact that I am not only an ambassador of my company, but also of my team, and even my specific role.

I will say "thank you" often. Not just at the end of the transaction, but also at the beginning.

I will genuinely ask "Is there anything more I can do for you?" before I conclude a transaction.

I will continuously look for opportunities to learn and improve my craft.

I will work every day to transcend what my job and customers expect of me.

My job is nothing without you.

ACTIVITY: My Job Is Nothing Without You

1. How does your job impact your Customers?

_____

_____

_____

_____

_____

_____

2. What excuses do you use that keeps you from providing better service to your Customers? On a separate sheet of paper, write those down, "I will stop doing…" and hang it somewhere you can see it every day.

16. The Key To Consistent Service

Do all customers deserve great service? What about those who always find something to complain about? How about those who never tip...or never say "thank you" ...or never seem to smile, ever? Up to this point, most of my writing, consulting, and training have always been based on the premise that all customers *deserve* the best we have to offer. After a recent encounter, however, my eyes are now open and I understand a very important truth that I never fully grasped before. At some point, we have to realize that our motivation to provide exceptional service cannot be based on the customer or whether he or she deserves it or not.

Grocery store cashier

Early, on a recent Sunday morning, I went up to my neighborhood grocery store to buy some items. Only two lines were open. After all, it was before 8AM on a Sunday morning. The line that I went in was staffed by a cashier who was prompt, thorough and engaging at the same time. When it was my turn, I couldn't help but thank her for being so wonderful to all of her customers. (Now here's the good part). She graciously thanked me, and then said "Well, I am not doing this for me. I'm not even doing this for the store. I'm doing it for him... (she pointed skyward). I HAVE TO serve with excellence because He serves us with excellence every day". Wow.

The implication immediately hit me. Her motivation to serve with excellence was not based on customers. In fact, it didn't really matter who the customers were. She was going to be exceptional anyway.

The Source

If we are being really honest, not all customers are enjoyable to serve. As professionals, however, we are supposed to be consistent, and our consistency cannot waiver. This means that our motivation has to be intrinsic and rooted in something that is firm and does not change. For the cashier, her source was a spiritual one. Your source could be

"By seeking to find the source to base your motivation on, you may find an additional reserve that you were unaware of."

that you are grateful for waking up every day. Or your source may be that you think of your children and hope to be a model that they can shape their lives after. Or perhaps you think of a deceased relative or friend or teacher or coach who was ALWAYS kind to you, and you strive to honor that person through how you serve others.

By seeking to find a source to base your motivation on, you may find an additional reserve that you were unaware of.

The Most Important Number

The last person you serve at the end of your shift, should not feel like they are the last person being served at the end of your shift. Period.

Sometimes, as we strive to please ALL customers, we forget how important ONE customer is. We may unintentionally dismiss or disregard the relevance of one customer. But that single customer may decide to tell many other friends and family members about the business. Plus, through the power of social media (Facebook, Twitter, Yelp, Travelocity, YouTube, etc.), countless more can either be turned off or turned on to your company.

Each day, at each touchpoint, strive to make each customer feel cherished. Not because of potential future business, but because of how much you are grateful for being in a position to serve others. And because you are grateful, you will not allow yourself to give anything less than your absolute best…regardless if your customer deserves it or not.

ACTIVITY: The Key to Consistent Service

Make a list of your daily Customer Touchpoints. Write down what you can do differently, better, or keep doing that will make the customer feel cherished?

Touchpoint	What will you do differently or better?

17. The Double Platinum Rule 2.0: Inform & Inspire

When I wrote the Double Platinum Rule years ago, my intent was to communicate the importance of exceeding customer expectations. To exceed expectations, you must not only treat people the way they want to be treated (Platinum Rule), but treat people the way they don't even know they want to be treated (Double-Platinum Rule). Then, something recently hit me. Many people may think that the double-platinum Rule is only about anticipating needs. It is not. The double-platinum rule is also about providing information that the customer may not have known otherwise. In other words, the true essence of the double-platinum rule is to add value to someone else's life beyond the basic service transaction.

> *"...it is about providing information that the customer may not have known otherwise."*

Example 1: I enjoy getting massages. I've been to many exquisite spas throughout the world, and have received countless massages. On a recent trip to the luxurious Kohler Waters Spa in Kohler, WI, the spa director told me something that I never heard before. She said that one of the best things I could do is to spend approximately 10 minutes in a steam room or sauna immediately before getting a massage. The purpose is so that my muscles could be nice and relaxed. This would allow the therapist to effectively massage my muscles (instead of spending precious time trying to loosen up the muscles first). I will take that piece of advice with me for the rest of my life. From now on, every massage I get will be preceded by me spending time in a steam room or sauna. The spa director informed and inspired me with knowledge that I did not know otherwise.

Example 2: Recently, I was at the local post office in my neighborhood, and saw a man struggling with multiple boxes while trying to open the front door at the same time. I immediately went to assist him. After thanking me, he mentioned that he hates the weekly chore of bringing all of his packages to the post office (he mentioned that he runs an eBay home business). I then explained that he could actually stay at home, go online, print the postage and schedule the packages to be picked up from his house. He was in utter amazement that such a service existed. Then, he became slightly irritated that no one at the post office had ever told him about the services I had just described.

Example 3: Just recently, I was on the phone with Korean Air to finalize a trip to Southeast Asia from Washington DC. Although my ticket was purchased online, I had to call Korean Air to purchase the plane ticket for my baby daughter. The customer service representative promptly inquired if I would like to order baby food for my daughter. I said, "Of course! I didn't even know that airlines offered baby food". She then explained that my baby's food would be delivered at the same time as everyone else's meals. Wow. The airline rep then asked if I would like to request an airline bassinet seat. "What's an airline bassinet seat?", I asked. She explained that it was a bassinet that my daughter can sleep in so she wouldn't have to be held for the entire trip. Again, wow. I did not know that such products or services existed.

To enliven the double-platinum rule, ask yourself this question: **What products and/or services does my company offer that some customers may not know about?** Then, starting today, begin listening intently to your customers...not only to what they are saying, but also listen to their mood and what they are hoping to achieve. The Kohler Waters Spa director listened to how much I enjoyed massages and used that as an opportunity to help enhance my massage experience from that point forward. The Korean Air customer service rep learned that I would be traveling with my daughter and immediately informed me about the airline's baby food and bassinet seat options. In the post office, I listened to a fellow customer's weekly disdain for bringing packages to the post office. I used that as an opportunity to inform him about the post office's various at-home options. In all three examples, someone was informed and inspired. That is the essence of the double-platinum rule.

> *"...but also listen to their mood and what they are hoping to achieve."*

Contrary to what many people think, wowing customers does not have to be an expensive task. Many times a WOW moment may not cost anything. Look for ways to wow daily. The key word is *daily*. Behaviors become habits when they are done every day (preferably multiple times per day). To inform and inspire is to add value to someone else's life. The double-platinum rule is about providing knowledge that someone can take with them. Above all, strive to make the double-platinum Rule your own minimum expectation for exceeding your customer's expectations, and the WOW moments will come naturally.

ACTIVITY: The Double Platinum Rule 2.0: Inform & Inspire

1. What products and/or services does your company offer that some customers may not know about?

_____

_____

_____

_____

_____

_____

2. How will you be able to inform and inspire your customers?

_____

_____

_____

_____

_____

18. The Professional's Pledge

From this day forth, I will be ashamed if I intentionally give anything less than my best. I have value, and was not put on this earth to begrudgingly exist. No, I was put here to make a meaningful and positive difference in the lives of others. Every book I've read, every class I've attended, and every lesson I've learned was not for me alone. I was blessed with such knowledge so I may use it to bless others. Otherwise, if I keep it to myself, I am being selfish. Yes, I am being unprofessional.

To be professional is what I am called to be. To take pride in my work is what I am called to do. Henceforth, I will always do more than is expected of me. I will not rely on my mood of the day to dictate how I go about my work. Like the wind, my mood will shift. Consistency cannot...must not shift. And professionals are consistent.

> *"My work is my brand. How I make others feel is my brand."*

My work is my brand. How I make others feel is my brand. The manner in which I do my work is my brand. Each morning when I awake, I will be grateful for yet another day to make a positive contribution to the world. Each night, when I'm in bed, I will assess my day to see if anyone's day was any better because of some contribution I made. The contribution can be as simple as opening a door for someone or giving a kind word to a stranger. The door that I opened may be the only kind deed that person experienced all year. That kind word to a stranger, may have helped rescue someone from a state of depression.

As a professional, I will not measure my success by the compensation or gratitude I receive from who I served. To do that is to set myself up for failure and heartache, because not every good deed will be acknowledged. Instead, I will give and serve because I demand that love pervades the very intention of my actions. Whatever my job may be, let me perform it with love, and I will not fail.

Beginning today, I will read these words, and they will help me re-focus on how precious this day truly is:

Today... enthusiastically and gratefully celebrate that I woke up.

Today...begin by loving myself, then let that same love guide how I treat others (regardless if they deserve it or not).

Today...do one thing for one customer, with absolute perfection...then repeat.

Today...tell one colleague that I value them and why.

Today...tell one customer that I value them and why.

Today...tell myself that I value myself and why.

Today...serve each person with excellence and not adjust my eagerness, kindness or attentiveness based on how "important" I believe a particular customer is.

Today...make it my minimum expectation to exceed everyone else's expectations.

Today...don't just serve...don't just engage...but truly honor each person I serve.

Today...graciously appreciate that no one else in the world can serve exactly like me, and be proud of that difference.

And when the day comes to a close, ask myself, "Did I make a positive, meaningful, and memorable difference in anyone's life today?"

Yesterday is gone. Tomorrow is not promised. All I have is today. And if I do nothing else, I will ensure that on this day, the world will know I am here.

ACTIVITY: The Professional's Pledge

In order to live up to the Professionals Pledge, commit to what you will need to Start, Stop and Continue to be the professional you are meant to be.

I will start…	
I will stop…	
I will continue…	

19. The LOVE Business

Martin Luther King, Jr. once said,

> *"Everybody can be great, because anybody can serve. You don't have to have a college degree to serve. You don't have to make your subject and verb agree to serve. You don't need to know about Plato and Aristotle to serve. You don't even need to know Einstein's theory of relativity to serve. You only need a heart full of grace. A soul generated by love."*

"...customers want to know that whoever happens to be serving them cares about their well-being."

Ladies and gentlemen, if you are serving others, then you are in the love business. To love means 'to care deeply for', and every customer, on some level, wants to be cared for. Whether it's in an airport, hospital, hotel, nursing home, spa, train or restaurant, customers want to know that whoever happens to be serving them cares about their well-being.

Yes, hotel guests appreciate luxurious room accommodations, but what they are really paying for is assurance that the staff will care enough to be attentive and look for ways to create exceptional memories for them. Yes, pharmacy customers expect to receive correct medications, but they also want the pharmacist to care enough to explain how to use the medication properly and any side effects. Yes, hospital and long-term care patients expect the medical team to help them feel better but, deep down, they also want to know that you will not treat them as just another patient in their already-busy day. People want...no...people yearn and crave to be loved. They need it.

The kind word you say to the customer; may be the only kind word they have heard all day...or all week...or all month. You don't know what their personal circumstances are. The man you are serving could have only a few weeks to live and he now finds himself being served by you. A woman could be having the worst year of her life for various reasons, and she now finds herself in your spa, your restaurant, your airline, or your bus. Your genuine smile may be the catalyst to turn her day completely around. In the end, money can buy material possessions, but memories and how we feel are all we have.

First Class

Those who truly understand what it means to infuse love into service don't classify their customers according to status. In other words, they don't serve VIP's "better" than everyone else. On the contrary, they serve everyone like

> *"First-class is not a section on an airplane; it is a mentality towards how you serve people."*

they are VIP's. Flight attendants who understand this concept shun the idea that those flying in first class should be treated *nicer*. No, these professionals treat every passenger as if they are in first-class. First-class is not a section on an airplane; it is a mentality towards how you serve people.

I was recently on a Delta flight, and experienced my first ever, **flight within a flight experience**. That is the only way I can describe the service that I received. Scott, the flight attendant, made every passenger in his assigned section of the plane feel incredibly valued and appreciated. Here's what Scott did:

- He proactively approached passengers to greet them as they entered his section (which I believe were rows 21 – 30).

- He welcomed them and asked, "Where are you sitting today?"

- He escorted the passengers to their seats, then offered to assist with putting their luggage in the overhead compartment.

- He wished each person an enjoyable flight.

Once I got situated in my seat, Scott noticed that I had pulled out a Delta coupon to redeem for a complimentary alcoholic beverage. He asked if this was my last flight of the day. When I told him that I actually had one more flight to catch, he told me, "Keep the coupon to use on your next flight today. Your drink on this flight is on me. I would like to make your entire flight experience with us today a memorable one." Nice.

And it gets better…

When he was preparing to serve beverages, he approached each passenger in his section and said, "We have some complimentary napkins for you." When I ordered the red wine, he said, "Excellent choice! We have our finest red wine for you from our cellar that has been aged just right." It was obvious to me that Scott took pride in ensuring that every passenger in his section had a memorable experience. He is the embodiment of *working like you own it*. Scott knows that he is in the love business.

Jessica the server

I recently visited the Grand Hotel Stockholm and the entire staff was very hospitable. They exuded professionalism and, more importantly, a genuine interest in my well-being while in their city. One evening, I went to one of the hotel's restaurants for dinner and was privileged to meet one of the finest servers in the world. Not only was she flawless with each of the various touchpoints, but she obviously loved her job. Jessica took great pride in honing her craft. She was proud of being a server. Actually, she loved being a server.

Jessica didn't just greet me…she welcomed me into her "home". She didn't just take my food and drink order…she shared her favorite menu items. When the food was delivered to the table, she did not just say, "enjoy your meal", she took a moment to explain everything on the plate. Jessica even gave a brief story about the ingredients, and where they came from (for each dish). The vegetables came from this place… the fish came from that place. As a diner, I felt an intimate connection with the food I was enjoying because she painted such a wonderful picture! Jessica knows that she is in the love business.

Let love manifest itself in how you speak, act and serve others. Your customers can, and will, feel it. They may not always tell you, but trust me, they appreciate it. In fact, the very act of genuinely serving IS love.

One of the best parts about being in the love business is its universal appeal. Everyone understands it on some level, and there is powerful karma associated with giving love. It always seems to find its way back to you. An ancient Chinese proverb notes, "a little bit of fragrance always clings to the hand that gives you roses". In this article's context, think of the roses as the service that you provide to others. And think of the fragrance as the inner peace and outer fulfillment that you have as a result of serving others. Ladies and gentlemen, we are in the love business.

ACTIVITY: The LOVE Business

1. Have your team tell a story: How do you show LOVE to your customers?
    Write your own story below.

    _____

    _____

    _____

    _____

    _____

2. Have Team Members send you their story in electronic form. Each day send
    your team a "The LOVE Business" email and attach one story.

20. The Most Important Thing

I have two confessions to make. One is…I am a huge fan of Zappos.com. So much so that I am dedicating a large chunk of this article to their renowned service culture. Every time I meet someone who has shopped at Zappos.com, the reaction is always the same, "I love Zappos!", "They are the best", etc. For those who don't know, Zappos.com is a successful online shoe and apparel retailer. My second confession is, as this article is being written (June 27, 2011), I have never actually shopped at Zappos.com, although I intend to whenever I get a moment. In case you are wondering why I seem to be such a staunch advocate of their brand without personally shopping their yet, the answer is simple. They understand the most important ingredient needed in order to build a world-class service culture.

> *"If your goal is to create an iconic and renowned service culture in your company, then service must be The Most Important Thing Your Company Does."*

Here it is: If your goal is to create an iconic and renowned service culture in your company, then service must be **The Most Important Thing Your Company Does**. Now, I don't mean that you work in a restaurant company that provides great service, or a nursing home that provides great service. I mean that, instead, you work in a great service company that operates restaurants or a great service company that runs nursing homes. The paradigm shift for those who truly understand (or "get it") is monumental. I worked at the Ritz-Carlton Hotel Company from 1996-2006, and throughout most of my time there, the senior leaders were emphatic that we were, first and foremost, a "service company". A service company that happened to manage hotels, restaurants and spas. The same is true for Zappos.com. That mindset pervades everything about their business from how they treat their employees to how they serve their customers. It even translates to how they relate with their vendors (vendor appreciation parties and other perks)!

So, the fundamental questions in this article are:

- What would happen if service excellence becomes the **Most Important Thing** your company does?

- How will your workforce see and feel the new emphasis on service?

- How will your customers see and feel the new emphasis on service?

- How would your hiring and orientation processes change?

- How would the selection of services your company offers change?

- How would the delivery of those services change?

Tony Hseig is the CEO of Zappos.com and in his book, "Delivering Happiness", he recounted the exact moment that he and his team decided that service would be the **Most Important Thing** they would do.

He wrote, *"Even though it would hurt our growth, we decided to cut most of our marketing expenses, and refocused our efforts on trying to get the customers who had already bought from us to purchase again and more frequently. Little did we know that this was actually a blessing in disguise, as it forced us to focus more on delivering better customer service. In 2003, we would decide to make customer service the focus of the company."*

Tony went on to explain, *"Our philosophy has been to take most of the money we would have spent on paid advertising and invest it into customer service and the customer experience instead, letting our customers do the marketing for us through word-of-mouth".* After reading that passage, I began to wonder about how powerful it would be if businesses truly understood the positive ramifications of that quote.

All this sounds good, but you are probably wondering how this shift can manifest itself into customer-focused service processes. Here is one of many examples from Zappos.com (also from the book, Delivering Happiness).

"An example of us using the telephone as a branding device is what happens when a customer calls looking for a specific style of shoes in a specific size that we're out of stock on. In those instances, every rep is trained to research at least three competitors' websites, and if the shoe is found in stock to direct the customer to the competitor. Obviously, in those situations, we lose the sale. But we're not trying to maximize each and every transaction. Instead, we're trying to build a lifelong relationship with each customer, one phone call at a time."

Hopefully, the message is resonating with you by now...the most effective way to build a service culture is to clearly make service the **Most Important Thing** your company does. Of course, you still have to execute your core business flawlessly whether it's a spa, hospital, or an airline. Massages, clinical procedures, and landing airplanes still must be done with excellence.

"There is something special about taking service seriously."

In the Washington DC metro area, there is a chain of grocery stores called "MOM's Organic Market". While their company mission is to protect and restore the environment, it is obvious that providing exceptional service is vital to their business success. We are fortunate to have a MOM's store not far from where we live, and I try to visit at least a few times per month. Recently, I decided to visit the store to buy a brand of organic milk. It was around 8:20AM, so I assumed that the store was already open.

When I arrived to the store, however, the sliding glass doors at the entrance didn't open (gasp!). I then looked at the hours of operation on the front door and it clearly stated that the store opens at 9AM. Before I could turn to walk away, a store employee came rushing to the front door, unlocked it, opened it and gave me a big "Good Morning! Come on in." I was a bit confused, but delighted at the same time. Then when I actually got inside, I noticed that there were at least two other shoppers already picking up groceries. Of course, I had to ask the store employee why the store opened before 9AM, and he said, "Because we try to open as early as possible to accommodate those customers who need to stop in before they go to work. By the way, please watch your step because we are still mopping and getting prepared to officially open at 9." Wow.

After I commented to him how impressed I was with the store's service-centric philosophy, he went on to tell me that just yesterday, one elderly shopper forgot her credit card at the cash register. One of the store employees knew where she lived in the neighborhood and volunteered to take it to her house. Wow times two!

There is something special about taking service seriously. It is important to honor that all people crave to feel appreciated and taken care of. By declaring (not suggesting, recommending or inferring), but steadfastly declaring that service is WHAT WE DO, you are automatically separating your company from the competition. Those exceptional service companies will be the ones that will continue to increase their market share, retain their best employees and win over the hearts of their customers. Is service THE MOST important thing you do?

ACTIVITY: The Most Important Thing

Take the time to reflect on the fundamental questions so that you can begin to see your organization as a "service provider" first and foremost.

What would happen if service excellence becomes the **Most Important Thing** your company does?	
How will your workforce see and feel the new emphasis on service?	
How will your customers see and feel the new emphasis on service?	
How would your hiring and orientation processes change?	

How would the selection of services your company offers change?	
How would the delivery of those services change?	

21. The Next Level in Service Excellence: Give. Share. Teach.

"Treat others the way they don't even know they want to be treated."

No matter how you look at it, serving is about giving. In fact, giving, sharing, helping and teaching all go hand-in-hand. When I wrote **The Double-Platinum Rule**, my intent was to highlight the importance of going beyond merely meeting expectations. I wanted to emphasize the importance of looking for opportunities to exceed customer expectations. In fact, The Double-Platinum Rule is *treat others the way they don't even know they want to be treated*. I believe, however, that there is a much bigger opportunity to capture the hearts and minds of our customers that transcends "exceeding expectations". The bigger opportunity that I'm referring to has to do with giving, sharing and teaching something to your customers. Share your subject matter expertise without expecting anything in return. By doing so, you can add immeasurable value to your team, your profession, and your customer's loyalty to the organization. Simply put - Give. Share. Teach.

Bow Ties

Recently, I visited the lovely MacArthur Place Hotel & Spa in Sonoma, CA. While there, I noticed that the food & beverage director always wore impeccable bow ties. Since I have always wanted to learn how to tie one, I asked him if he would mind teaching me before I left. However, since my schedule was so full during my hotel stay, I never had the time to meet with him. On the day of my checkout, a bellman brought a bag to my room, which contained…(you guessed it)…a new (and dapper) bow tie! There were also *step by step instructions* (with illustrations) on how to properly tie a bow tie. He also called me a few days later to see if I had any questions about tying the perfect bow tie. *Give. Share. Teach.*

Winery

During another trip to Sonoma, I had the opportunity to visit a few wineries for wine tastings. One of the wineries was called Artesa Vineyards & Winery and was located in the Carneros region between Sonoma and Napa Valley. The wine tasting consisted of four different wines. There was Sauvignon Blanc,

Chardonnay, Merlot, and Cabernet Franc. Up until that point, I had heard of Cabernet Franc, but didn't know much else about that particular grape. When I inquired with the wine server, he explained that Cabernet Franc is one of the parents of the more famous Cabernet Sauvignon. In fact, he continued, "long ago, Cabernet Franc fell in love with Sauvignon Blanc and the offspring was Cabernet Sauvignon". He also gave me a printed document with additional information about the Cabernet Franc and its history. *Give. Share. Teach.*

Allergies

Since moving to the Washington DC metro area in 2004, I have been experiencing allergy-related symptoms during the springtime (allergy season). So each year, I would make the pilgrimage to my pulmonologist, who would listen to my lungs, hear me cough, check my throat, and eventually, prescribe allergy medications that would help me get better. This year, however, my wife (who also happens to be the VP of Medical Affairs for our household) suggested that I use a pro-active approach. Rather than passively wait for my allergy symptoms to reach an unbearable level, she recommended that I see the doctor before allergy season began, get the medications, and begin taking them daily to keep the symptoms at bay.

So that is exactly what I did. I went to the doctor's office, explained my strategy (or rather my wife's strategy), and something interesting happened. He said, "I agree. One of the best ways to avoid suffering any allergy infections is to preemptively take the medications daily during allergy season." At that moment, I tried to maintain my composure, because I wanted to blurt out, "Then why didn't you tell me this years ago!!!" *Give. Share. Teach.*

> *"The true power in the human element of service excellence is how you make someone feel."*

It is never enough to comply with requests. Some people approach customer service like this: Take a request, comply with the request, repeat. Take a request, comply with the request, repeat. Kiosks can do the same thing. Don't be a kiosk.

The true power in the human element of service excellence is how you make someone feel. As a result of being served by you, people should literally feel better about themselves. In fact, they should feel engaged, inspired and renewed!

So don't just comply...anticipate needs. And don't just anticipate needs...teach something. Add value to your customers' lives by giving and teaching something that they didn't realize they were missing. When you are able to do that consistently, then service becomes much more than a chore, or something that "you don't mind doing". It becomes a privilege and an honor. Knowing that you have made a positive difference in the life of someone else is truly what service is all about. Give. Share. Teach.

Supplement:

Here are some action steps that you can use to implement the "Give.Share.Teach." service method.

1. First, understand and appreciate that you are a subject matter expert in *some aspect* of your role, company, and/or industry.

2. Identify at least one or two things that you can share with your customers (that they may not already know).

3. Brainstorm with your team about their subject matter expertise.

4. Select a few things that your team can give, share, and teach.

5. Prepare learning "take-away" that you can give to your customers (i.e., a handout, website, book recommendations, etc.)

6. Always ask your customers if there is additional information that they would like to know. This last step can be a great way to identify new things to Give. Share. Teach.

ACTIVITY: The Next Level in Service Excellence: Give. Share. Teach

Commit to building this next level of service by creating an action plan to implement "Give. Share. Teach."

Action	By When?	Notes
Make a list of the knowledge and skills you have that make you an expert at what you do.		
Identify at least one or two things that you can share with your customers (that they may not already know).		
Brainstorm with your team about their subject matter expertise.		
Select a few things that your team can give, share, and teach.		
Prepare learning "take-away" that you can give to your customers (i.e., a handout, website, book recommendations, etc.)		

22. A Patient's Plea

*This article is based on my real events, and it is my hope that everyone, in any industry, will be able to find nuggets of learning throughout.

(My voice) To the clinic receptionist:

Just who do you think you are? I don't even want to be here and your indifferent demeanor is clearly saying "I am doing YOU a favor". Visiting clinics like these make me mad and depressed at the same time. I am mad because I have to come here, but depressed that I couldn't somehow avoid being sick so I can COMPLETELY avoid people like you. At the "reception" desk. What a joke. There was nothing receptive about how you didn't acknowledge anyone who entered through the automatic doors. There was nothing receptive about how you begrudgingly nodded to the stack of clipboards, and said, "Take one. Fill it out. Return it to me." There was nothing receptive about how you shouted "NEXT!!!!" Wow. I already don't feel well, and now I find myself completely reliant on the services that you and your team have. So while I want to tell you a piece of mind, I, like many others, will sit here patiently awaiting my turn to be called by the Triage Nurse. Although there may not be any proof to back it up, I can't help but think that if I said something to you, that you might "mistakenly forget" to pass along my paperwork to the triage nurse; thus, extending my time in the waiting area. So instead, I will just wait and hope that I never have to come back here to see people like you again. But chances are, inevitably, I will have to.

> *"In many ways, who you allow to be in that role (receptionist) will speak volumes about your organization's commitment to service excellence."*

The sad part is that even though that receptionist was obviously in the wrong role, I'm confident that she knows HOW to be receptive and congenial. I'm sure that if I was her long-lost friend or favorite relative who came through the entry doors, the greeting would have been MUCH different. Even more than that, the feeling and emotion behind the greeting would have been much different as well. I would have felt welcomed, listened to, guided and empathized with.

Lesson: Ensure that you have the right person in the receptionist role. That person is absolutely crucial to the overall success of your service operation. In fact, regardless of what your company's mission statement declares about service, all one has to do is observe and/or listen to the first point of contact for your business. In many ways, who you allow to be in that role will speak volumes about your organization's commitment to service excellence.

(My voice) To the Triage nurse and Physician

So, I've been escorted to this patient room, told to sit on the bed, and wait for the nurse. Um, did they forget that I was in here? It's been at least 30 minutes, and no one's come by to check on me or anything. Maybe they are on a lunch break. But, oh wait, it's 9:36AM. Too early for a lunch break. Now, don't get me wrong. I expect to wait. Waiting isn't really the ISSUE. The real issue is being kept informed about the wait time. Someone, somewhere, in this clinic can tell me something about when I can expect for a nurse (or any other human) to visit me. Compounding matters even more, there was a sign on the wall (in my patient room), that listed a set of seven service standards. The first three were:

We will make every effort to:

* Introduce you to our team

* Inform you and your family of your plan of care

* Update you regularly on your procedure times and delays (yeah, I had to read that one twice)

The triage nurse showed up, with no smile, no eye contact. Just started asking/reading a list of standard questions to me, then proceeded with the typical blood pressure exam and inserting the thermometer under my tongue. I kept thinking, WOW, a robot can possibly do her job...at the level she was doing it.

I explained my ailment to the nurse, she took notes on her computer, then left. Next (well actually, approximately 25 minutes later), the physician came in and asked what was the reason for my visit. What?! I'm thinking, "didn't the nurse relay that information to you?" Based on the follow-up questions, it was clear that he and the nurse had not communicated at all. Very comforting, indeed (I'm being sarcastic). Seriously, I don't know you, but I'm hoping (praying, wishing) that you know what you are doing. Plus, I trust that you (the physician) and the nurse will communicate and work together for the benefit of my health.

At the absolute basic level, patients expect their healthcare providers to be competent and informed. Not everyone is necessarily meant to be in a job that serves others. Indeed, it takes a special person to enjoy serving people. It takes an even more special person to enjoy serving people in a healthcare environment. I strongly believe that healthcare professionals (especially nurses), have no right to view their work as "just a job". No way! Too many people rely on them, and what they do is far too meaningful, relevant and life-altering.

Lesson: Continuously help your team members re-orient themselves with the purpose of their role. The purpose is much more than fulfilling a set of tasks or functions. It is almost immoral to hire someone to fulfill a function. Instead, invite people to be a part of your organization's family. Share your company's dreams with them. Help each employee continuously hone a sense of purpose and relevance for their role.

That receptionist was not JUST a receptionist. She was the person who should have been warm, welcoming and helped to alleviate some of the typical anxiety that many people have.

That triage nurse was more than someone who took my vitals. She should have been empathetic, warm and re-assuring that I would feel better.

That physician is more than just someone who examines me, diagnoses my ailment and writes a prescription. He should have spoken with the nurse to ascertain what my specific issue was. Then come into the room informed and eager to assist.

As I was writing the lessons for each section of this article, I noticed that none of them necessarily required any extra money to be spent by the organization. All they require is for caring and attentive people to give what they can with what they have. If I may leave you with one takeaway from this article, it is this: Make service excellence the most important thing on your team and everything else will fall into place. If service excellence is important, then you will regularly talk about it, recognize it, and chastise it (when it's not done). Some of the most beautiful and inspiring service I've seen has taken place in a healthcare setting. It is a special honor to be a blessing to patients and their families. If I have one wish today, it would be for everyone working in healthcare to view their roles in a renewed light. Not because they were told to…but because the patients and their families deserve it.

ACTIVITY: A Patient's Plea

Take an honest assessment of the customer experience in your business. List the major touchpoints a customer experiences when they do business with you. Keep in mind that is some cases a major touchpoint could even be on the phone.

For each touchpoint, use the table provided and note your expectations, along with ways you can exceed those expectations, and then observe several customer interactions at that touchpoint. Reward, or coach, your team on how well they meet those expectations.

Touchpoint	Expectations	Exceeding the Expectation
1.		
2.		
3.		
4.		
5.		
6.		
7.		
8.		
9.		
10.		

23. Can you MAKE Your Team Work Like They Own It?

"Train Me...not to just meet expectations, but to exceed them; Empower Me...to do the right thing in any situation; Tell Me...how I am doing."

"How can I make my employees work like they own it?" That is the question I often get from well-meaning leaders who hope to create a strong service culture. Well, the honest answer is that you really can't MAKE anyone work like they own it. You can, however, create an environment where they want to. After all that I've written concerning this topic, I would like to outline, from the employee's perspective, the access code needed to unlock your staff's desire to work with an ownership mentality. Let us begin with a doorman in Geneva...

The Doorman

On a recent trip to the lovely city of Geneva, I stayed at the Beau-Rivage hotel, and was thoroughly impressed with a particular doorman. He was the embodiment of the word REFINED. Everything from his upright posture, to the way he walked with a sense of purpose exuded that he took great pride in his work. I noticed him removing cigar butts from the sidewalk, checking potted plants for trash and giving a hearty "Welcome back!" or "Enjoy your day!" (to guests and random people walking by the hotel). In short, he was working like he owned it, but it was also obvious that no one was MAKING him do so. Of course, personal motivation may be a factor along with his upbringing; however, I would like to highlight three keys that make up the access code that can unlock the desire to work like you own it.

Train Me...to not just meet, but exceed expectations

From the very beginning, every employee needs to know that merely adhering to standards (no matter how grand) is not their job. Their real job is to intentionally and consistently look for opportunities to surprise and delight. Here's an example of a touchpoint table that I put together for this chapter:

Touchpoint	Meet Expectations	Exceed Expectations
Asking the concierge for a restaurant recommendation.	Concierge provides a restaurant name and contact information. Also offers to call and make a reservation for the guest.	Concierge goes online and prints the restaurant menu and proactively offers ground transportation (and/or driving directions). If the concierge has been to the restaurant, he/she can recommend certain dishes, etc.
Visitor coming to see an inpatient in a hospital.	Nurse greets the visitor.	Nurse finds out the visitor's name and approximate time of arrival from the patient. Then, when visitor comes, the nurse greets him/her by name. If it's multiple visitors, the nurse can have additional chairs in the room with extra cups for water. If the nurse knows that little kids will be coming, then have appropriate toys available.

Once the touchpoint table is done, focus on one touchpoint per week (or one per day if you are feeling ambitious). Role-play, discuss, and notice when the staff is (or is not) adhering to the standards; then, give feedback accordingly. The goal is to focus on exceeding expectations. If you want your team to exceed expectations every, then you have to talk about exceeding expectations every day.

Empower Me...to do the right thing in any situation

Saying "You are empowered" is not enough. There is a very real possibility that your employees have never worked at a place where they have been empowered. So regularly share examples of when the staff (and even you) have used empowerment to surprise and delight customers. Go on our **Work Like You Own It!** site and share those stories as well. Customers judge the quality of your business by the responsiveness of the first person they come in contact with to address their issue. Once your staff feels empowered, your job is to then encourage it...on a daily basis. Since empowerment really is about "caring enough" to do something, it is important to celebrate the "caring" just as much (if not more so) as the empowerment act itself.

When I was a front desk agent, a guest called to say that their toilet was overflowing, so I empowered myself to comp their $700/night room for the remaining three nights of their stay. When my manager found out, she could have yelled at me for losing precious revenue, but that would have only crushed my esteem and prevented me from empowering myself again. Instead, she said "Thank you for caring enough to do something". She then seized that opportunity as a teachable moment and said, "Now, let's discuss some other ways to handle similar situations in the future". I was re-assured that I did the right thing by taking action and learned ways to better handle similar situations in the future.

Tell me...how I am doing

Your team craves feedback. It is like oxygen for the body. When there is no feedback, performance suffers. Feedback can be positive, constructive or negative. Positive feedback (aka recognition) is intended to let the recipients know that their hard work is, in fact, appreciated. Make no mistake, people who work hard need to know that their hard work is not taken for granted. Of course, everyone wants recognition in their own way (public, private, written, verbal, etc.).

Constructive feedback, however, is letting your employees know when their performance did not meet the expected standard of performance. It is very possible for an employee to do their job improperly and not know because no one ever says anything. It is also possible for an employee to intentionally make shortcuts in their work, and the lack of management feedback is a green light that the shortcut is OK. One best practice is to start with the standard, then describe the employee's action that did not meet the standard. At this point, the performance gap should be self-evident to the employee. Finally, explain why the standard is so important and why the employee's action was detrimental.

Explain to your team that one of the true hallmarks of being a professional is steady consistency. Regardless if it's busy or not. Or whether you have a headache or not...or even if your co-worker and/or boss is annoying you. True professionals have the uncanny ability to block out the "noise" and do what they are supposed to do, when they are supposed to do it, whether they feel like it or not. If you train, empower, and tell your team (how they are doing), they will be far more likely to own it, versus you hoping or mandating that they do so.

ACTIVITY: Can you MAKE Your Team Work Like They Own It?

If you are a supervisor, use the table below to identify what you need to train your team to; what you can empower them to do and how you can recognize them.

If you don't supervise people, use the table to identify what you want to be trained to do; what you would like to be empowered to do and how you want to be recognized and then share this with your supervisor.

Train Me	Empower Me	Tell Me

24. The Smile Reserve

"There is something beautiful about people who know there is no limit to their kindness."

Some people believe that they have a limited supply of kindness. After the first ten people, for example, their "smile reserve" will dry up, and there will be no more smiles for anyone else. Their "anticipate needs" reserve will be empty, and their "learn preferences" reserve will be depleted. They feel like they can't actually be nice to every customer they meet. It's not possible! Or is it?

Commuter flight

Recently, I was on board a small commuter plane that was staffed with one flight attendant. The first person to board the plane was an elderly lady, and I saw the attendant give her a warm hug and big smile before she boarded. When the other passengers boarded, however, there were no smiles for anyone else. In fact, there was barely any eye contact. The elderly lady was seated in the front row close to where the flight attendant was sitting, and the attendant smiled EVERY time she spoke with her. The other passengers got nothing of the sort.

We can reason that the attendant was nice to the elderly lady because she knew her. It was obvious that they had some type of relationship. Really, is it fair to expect the attendant to be as nice to perfect strangers as she is to someone she obviously knows?

Well, it was obvious that she knew HOW to smile and be hospitable. It was also obvious that she knew how to be warm and congenial. The attendant merely decided who she would be warm and congenial with.

There are those who reserve their smiles for:

- People who they know
- People who they find attractive
- People who are in their same age group
- People who are in their same race
- People who they perceive to be in their same socio-economic status

- People who they believe they can get something from (tips, job promotions, etc.)

If you are in the business of serving people, the assumption is that you actually like people. Regardless of the industry, the vast majority of people you serve will, in fact, be complete strangers. *This means that if you don't enjoy being nice to people you don't know, then you are probably in the wrong line of work.*

There is something beautiful about people who know there is no limit to their kindness. They know that their smiles won't, somehow, vanish when used often. They also know that by approaching service with love in their heart that customers will always feel genuinely cared for. They know that they can, and will, be nice to every person they serve. They will strive to learn the preferences of every person they serve. They will look to do more than the bare minimum with every person they serve. And the reason they will do this is because they...love...people; regardless if they know them, or if they find them attractive, or if they are in the same age group, or if they are in the same race, or if they are in the same socio-economic group, or if they believe they can get something from them.

So, my challenge to you (and myself) is to love people, period. And serve people, period. Then, everything else will take care of itself.

ACTIVITY: The Smile Reserve

One of the best ways to make improvements is to begin by taking an honest inventory of your current behaviors and beliefs. Once you have recognized what is driving your behavior you can begin to take steps for improvement. Use the table below to track what causes your behaviors and how you can make changes.

What causes your smile reserve to dry up?	
What can you do to change that from happening?	

25. The Three Ingredients of Engaging Service: Humility, Reverence, Professionalism

On a recent family trip to Bali, we had the privilege of flying on Korean Air. Virtually every touchpoint was memorable. Everything from the reservations process, to the actual flights, was world-class, and I was able to glean some key learning points to share with you. I am a firm believer that whenever you learn something, you should share it so that others may also benefit. The important thing is that any organization, in any industry, can take away something from this article to immediately apply.

> *"While some people believe that service is something that you do, I believe that service is something that you are."*

On the flights, I got the sense that nothing was more important to the staff than being attentive to our needs. There was a potent blend of humility, reverence and professionalism all at the same time. To be honest, I had never experienced that type of service before. The staff could not have been more confident…their shoes could not have been any shinier…and their smiles could not have been any brighter. While some people believe that service is something that you do, I believe that service is something that you are. You have to BE service. The Korean Air flight attendants **were** service.

Flight delay

Typically, when a flight is delayed, the captain makes a general announcement over the plane's speaker system. On our return trip to the U.S. we had to catch a connecting flight in Seoul, South Korea. After we were on the plane, each flight attendant went to their section of the plane and informed their passengers about a 1-hour flight delay. Now I don't mean a general announcement to their respective section. I mean that the flight attendant went row by row, looked the passengers in their eyes and empathetically informed them about the flight delay. Then after 30-minutes, the attendants went back around to give an update. When the flight was finally ready to depart, they went to their respective sections again and gave the *good news*.

Personalize

Flight attendants usually have a report that shows where passengers are seated, along with their names. Despite having this information, most attendants don't leverage this important data. At Korean Air, the attendants not only knew my name, but they welcomed my wife, our daughter and me by our names. Think of how many times you might know your customers' names and not use it to your advantage to create an inclusive and attentive experience.

Presentation

There are times when I have patronized a business and got the sense that the staff was not really engaged. To those types of employees, serving others is a temporary or part-time job until they find a "real" job. On Korean Air, I had no such feeling. Everyone had a sense of pride and honor as they went about their work. This professionalism was very apparent in how they presented everything. Let's start with the baby stroller.

On Korean Air, before you board the flight, one of the employees proactively greets you and offers stroller assistance. They explain the stroller check-in process and claim procedure. After you fold the stroller, the staff puts it in an elegant and transparent bag, then presents you with a claim check. When you get off the plane, a staff member proactively directs and/or escorts you to a waiting area (exclusively for parents waiting for their strollers). An employee brings you the stroller and wishes you an enjoyable day.

Service, in its purest sense, is about knowing that you have added value to someone else, regardless of the circumstance. The key phrase is "someone else". To do so effectively, you must have a sense of humility because you understand that service is not about the giver, it is about the recipient. With humility in mind, the next logical step is to show reverence for whomever you are serving. It is almost impossible to show reverence if you're not humble. The staff at Korean Air found joy in showing reverence to their passengers while being humble, yet confident enough to flawlessly deliver world-class service.

As I flew on Korean Air, I could not help but daydream of how great it would be if all businesses had a similar mindset and approach regarding customer service. To sum up my Korean Air experience, I will use three words: humility, reverence, and professionalism. My challenge to you is to design your customer service experience with those three words in mind and you will build your own legion of loyal customers.

ACTIVITY: The Three Ingredients of Engaging Service: Humility, Reverence, Professionalism

1. What can you do to personalize the service you provide? Create a list and then share your commitments with your supervisor (or peers).

_____

_____

_____

_____

_____

2. What makes you most proud of the service you provide? Share your notes with your supervisor (or peers) and discuss ways to demonstrate that pride on a regular basis.

_____

_____

_____

_____

26. Three Tips to Help Drive Repeat Business

> *"Customers can easily tell if you are revenue-driven vs. relationship-driven."*

People don't like to feel like they are a transaction. That is exactly how I felt when I recently rented a car. The rental car agent was fast and efficient. He spat out a series of standard car rental questions with laser-like proficiency. In fact, the entire transaction took less than three minutes. Speed = A+. Engagement = F. I remember walking away from the transaction saying "Wow, a robot could do that employee's job". It is important to note that people still like to feel like their patronage is valued.

In that car rental example, I did not feel valued; actually, it was quite obvious that the attendant cared very little about making me feel valued. In his mind, it was "on to the next one". To develop a strong service culture, we can never lose respect for the big "R": RELATIONSHIP. People (especially customers) thrive off of relationships. Customers can easily tell if you are revenue-driven vs. relationship-driven. Even if the service transaction is a very quick one, it is still possible to establish a relationship which can lead to higher customer engagement, loyalty, referrals and repeat business.

Pay Attention to What Your Customers Care About

It is amazing to see how many organizations implement all sorts of initiatives, without checking to see if those initiatives are actually important to their customers. For example, I have heard stories of hotels ironing newspapers! Those organizations that get it right, however, make a habit of regularly soliciting insight from their customers about what can further strengthen their relationship.

I was in Wegman's Supermarket recently and noticed the employees, who retrieve shopping carts from the parking lot, using a sanitary wipe to clean the carts' handle bars. I would imagine that there are many customers who care about that. I was walking around Washington DC's National Zoo recently during the summer, and there were water-misting stations strategically located throughout the zoo for patrons to get a quick cool-off. Customers care about that. I recently stayed at the Eventi hotel in New York City, and in my guest room closet there were not only the standard hotel slippers, but also socks.

Socks! Some guests, like me, prefer socks than slippers because my feet tend to get cold.

It is critical to not fall into the habit of assuming that you currently know and will always know what your customers want. It doesn't matter how many years you've been in your profession, or how many academic credentials you have. Your organization will only attain and maintain its competitive edge if it can accurately meet and exceed its customers' expectation better than its competitors.

Be Inclusive

"I want you to know me, care about me, and make me feel like an insider". That is the mantra of your loyal customers (and your *potentially* loyal customers). One of the biggest mistakes companies make is to reserve their loyal customer treatment for only **current** loyal customers. It's as if only those customers who have proven that they will return again, will be *rewarded* with VIP treatment. Here's a newsflash: If you want new customers to become loyal customers, then you have to treat them like loyal customers! I can certainly understand how some perks may only be available to long-term customers (or frequent buyers), but I'm referring to the sense of urgency and caring that are given.

On a recent trip, the airline gate attendant was getting ready to initiate the boarding process. She said something along the lines of, "Welcome to flight xxx. We are now ready to begin boarding. As always, we will board according to zones, and we value our elite customers." In case you missed it, here is the last part again, "We Value Our ELITE Customers". Now, I happen to be a so-called ELITE customer with this particular airline due to my frequent-flier status, but my first thought was…"don't you value everyone else??" Again, the idea is to create more loyal customers by treating every customer like a loyal customer (or at least make them feel like you *want* them to be a loyal customer).

Feeling included also means that you accept your customers for who they are, and not minimize your service to them due to such things as their age, race, or (perceived) socio-economic status. Accepting your customers also means that you do and say things that will lift them up, and not bring them down. A friend of mine recently visited a spa to get a massage. When she visited the spa, however, she happened to be in the midst of an acne breakout. When the massage therapist came to the massage room, she told my friend, "Oh my goodness! You have lots of acne!". #1) My friend already knew she had acne. #2) She felt embarrassed and self-conscious. Note: Customers should feel *better* as a result of interacting with you…not worse.

Be Appreciative and Grateful

What happens right after you provide a service or product to your customer? What about the day, week, or month after? You would be astonished to see how few companies have any type of standard regarding thanking their customers. Your customers just made a conscious decision to give you their business vs. giving it to another company. They should feel re-assured that their decision was the right one. In addition to verbally (and genuinely) thanking them for their business, consider doing the following *within the **first week** after the service*:

- Send a Handwritten Thank you-card (handwritten-cards are quickly becoming a lost art. Writing them will instantly help you and your organization stand apart from the competition)
- Send an Email – Specifically thanking your customers for their patronage, AND how much you look forward to serving them again.

Then, four weeks after the service:

- Make a follow-up phone call or email to see if they have any questions or would like additional information on how to best use or sustain the service/product. (Tip: do this step without asking for anything…i.e. sales pitches, etc.)

Your customers should eagerly rave about how wonderful your business is and how much they look forward to returning. This will only happen, however, if they feel like they are in a relationship with your business. I recently visited a friend's house, and overheard him say to someone, "Yeah, we've been together since 1993." I would have bet any amount of money that he was referring to a girlfriend. Not so, he was actually speaking about the consumer electronics company, *Crutchfield*. Wow. He absolutely loves Crutchfield. I have no doubt that if Crutchfield was a woman, he would propose immediately.

I firmly believe that customers would prefer to be loyal, rather than bouncing around from business to business. I even know people who begrudgingly tolerate mediocre service because they don't have the patience to look elsewhere.

> *"I firmly believe that customers would prefer to be loyal, rather than bouncing around from business to business."*

As a business seeking ways to cultivate a loyal customer base, you should make your customers feel celebrated…rather than tolerated. Pay attention to what your customers care about, be inclusive, and be appreciative. If you make a habit of practicing those three tips, your relationships will thrive and the revenue will follow.

ACTIVITY: Three Tips to Help Drive Repeat Business

1. How well do you know what your customers care about? Make a list of what you believe they care about and then meet with a few of your peers and discuss this question and share what you came up with. The purpose is to use this discussion to strengthen your knowledge of what your customers care about.

_____

_____

_____

_____

_____

2. How do your customers know that you care about them? Make a list of ways you believe you convey your appreciation. Meet with a few of your peers and discuss this question and share your perspective. Generate a discussion that results in identify additional ways to let your customers know that you appreciate them.

_____

_____

_____

_____

_____

27. Two of the Most Important Phrases in Service Excellence

Two of the most important phrases in service excellence are, "I don't know" and "Let me find out". As opposite as they may be, both phrases speak volumes about the service culture on a team. One wreaks of indifference and apathy, while the other expresses ownership and initiative. One of the words, has absolutely no business on a team where service is supposed to be paramount. The other should be the minimum standard that EVERYONE is held accountable to.

Banquet Server

"It's never OK to be half-way competent, on purpose. If you don't know something, find out."

Early in my hotel career, one of my jobs was as a banquet server. In that role, my job was to serve guests at catering events such as wedding receptions, holiday parties, etc. One evening, there was a large banquet in the hotel ballroom that began with light hors d'oeuvres (pronounced "awr durvz") during the welcome reception, followed by a formal dinner. So I retrieved my tray of hors d'oeuvres from the cook, without bothering to study what the items were. I figured that by merely glancing at them, I would *know enough* to explain to the guests what the items were.

Before I made it out to the ballroom, however, the chef stopped me and began quizzing me on the items on my tray. Of course, I did not know what they were. He looked me in the eyes and said, "You are not a professional ", then walked away. I was crushed. I then went back to the cook, who I retrieved the hors d'oeuvres from and learned how they were made, what were the ingredients and found out everything I could about each one. Before I went back to the ballroom, I found the chef and told him about each hors d'oeuvres. He looked at me again and said, "Now, you are a professional".

Takeaway: It's never ok to be half-way competent, on purpose. If you don't know something, find out.

Sushi

During a recent hotel stay, I was in the mood to eat sushi for dinner. So I asked a front desk employee about where I could find a nearby sushi restaurant. She said "I don't know", and left it at that. I went to another employee, Jake, who was a few feet away and asked the same question. He didn't know either but immediately went to find out. Jake then gave me two options that were less than five miles away. He then asked if I could wait a moment while he found out the exact address and hours of operation for each restaurant. Jake not only returned with these items, but also printed the menus for me.

Takeaway: Get excited about learning something new that can help the customer.

Indifference

It's one thing to not know. It's another to be *content* with not knowing. The front desk agent in the previous story was obviously satisfied with not knowing. Whenever I see an apathetic employee, the first thing that goes through my mind is…"You must have

> *"Never, EVER tolerate indifference on your team."*

a very poor manager who *allows* you to work here AND have an indifferent attitude". I saw a statistic once which showed that over 60% of customers stop patronizing a particular business because of an attitude of indifference on the part of a company employee.

Takeaway: All it takes is one employee to turn a customer away forever. Conversely, all it takes is one employee to turn a customer into a loyal ambassador of your business.

Make no mistake…people will do whatever you allow them to do (or not do). Inevitably, that indifferent attitude will get even worse (and infectious) when it becomes clear that the manager is not going to address it. On the other hand, morale soars when standards are high and expectations are clear.

Takeaway: Never, EVER tolerate indifference on your team.

Regularly share information with your team and ask them to come up with a list of "commonly asked questions" that your customers have. On a weekly basis, challenge everyone to share one thing they learned over the past week that could benefit the customer (and/or the team). While being knowledgeable is critical, there will be times when you honestly won't know the answer to a customer's question. It may seem simple, but offering to find out the answer PLUS giving a little more information can have a tremendous impact on the service experience. It shows that you care. As I've written previously, service really is about genuinely caring. No matter what the question or request is, as long as its legal, ethical, and moral, find out. Your customers will appreciate it, you will have pride in your job, and your team will develop a stellar reputation for being exceptional.

ACTIVITY: Two of the Most Important Phrases in Service Excellence

Track the most common customer questions. If you are a supervisor, meet with your team weekly to share the questions and discuss the answers. If you are not a supervisor, track the questions and take them to your supervisor to discuss.

Customer Question	Best Answer

28. Exceeding Your Customers Expectations? Why Bother?

"...the way you perceive your work has a major impact on whether you 'bother' to exceed expectations or not."

Let's be honest. Most people's paychecks will be exactly the same whether they meet or exceed their customers' expectations. Unless you work for one of those rare companies that provide financial incentives to go above and beyond, why go through the trouble of *doing more?* Seriously, doing more requires more effort, and more effort requires more time.

So, my question is, why bother? The answer may be found in how you view your work. Is it a job, a career or a calling? As we will see, the way you perceive your work has a major impact on whether you "bother" to exceed expectations or not.

Job. Career. Calling.

In Shawn Achor's book, *The Happiness Advantage*, he referred to a study that was done by one of his research colleagues. The study was focused on how people viewed *work*. It turns out that they either viewed work as a job, a career or a calling. Those who view work as a job, primarily see working as a way to pay bills. They rarely do more than the bare minimum. Those who view work as a career have a bit more vested interest, and aspire to have longevity via job promotions, transfers, etc. Finally, those who view work as a calling find intrinsic value in what they do. Their work is genuinely meaningful, and their pay is the proverbial "icing on the cake". There are doctors and lawyers who may view their work as a job, while there are housekeepers and truck drivers who see their work as a calling (and the opposite is also true of course).

Imagine two groups of administrative assistants who have the same experience, same education, and same supervisor. One group views their work as a job, while the other group sees it as a calling. The assistants, who see their work as "just a job" will do the bare minimum. In fact, anything above the bare minimum will be viewed as a chore. Any question or request will be perceived as an interruption of their day. Those assistants will complain when they receive "too many" emails or phone calls.

On the contrary, the administrative assistants who view their work as a calling will happily and eagerly look for opportunities to exceed expectations. They won't complain when they are busy. In fact, they will be happy when they are busy. The ringing phones and constant emails mean that their job is relevant and important. After all, if there are no customers, then why would their jobs exist? Most importantly, they are grateful because they have the opportunity to make a difference in someone's day…every day.

Molé (*pronounced Mo-Lay*)

On a recent trip to Salt Lake City, Utah, I was fortunate to visit a Mexican restaurant called The Red Iguana. The food was amazing and the service was equally impressive. One of the highlights occurred a short while after I was seated. The server welcomed me, introduced himself, then asked if it was my first trip to the restaurant. When I said yes, he welcomed me again, and explained some of the history and key features of the restaurant including their world famous molé sauce. He then told me about the various types of molé sauce and offered to bring samples of the sauces for me to try. I instantly fell in love with the sauce, and bought a pint to take home with me.

The server could have easily (and with much less effort), just taken my food order, and proceeded with merely meeting my expectations. My lunch experience could have been "just another meal" on "just another business trip". As we know, however, memorable service experiences are not created by people who meet expectations. They are created by people who exceed them.

"For those who view their work as a calling, exceeding is not really a bother at all."

Our original question was, "Why bother to exceed expectations?" The short answer is that for those who view their work as a calling, exceeding is not really a *bother* at all. It is an honor…rather a privilege to be of service. Some people mistakenly believe that exceeding expectations is a gradual step up from meeting expectations. It is not. They are actually two…different...things. If you want to exceed, then you must *intentionally* think of ways to exceed.

So, while your pay may be the same, the service you provide will be memorable, and the innate joy you experience will be priceless.

ACTIVITY: Why Bother Exceeding Your Customers Expectations

1. List five points of the service experience. For each point identify what the customer is likely to expect. Now, make a list of how you can exceed those expectations.

_____

_____

_____

_____

_____

2. What are some ways you can create an atmosphere of exceeding expectations?

_____

_____

_____

_____

_____

29. Earn and Re-Earn Your Customers' Loyalty

When I am traveling in the U.S., my favorite airline is Southwest Airlines. It is very obvious to me that Southwest understands that customer service is more than just a public relations statement. For example, they give you the option of having a customer service phone representative call you back instead of waiting on hold for a long time. Just recently, I had two business trips that required me to seek out other airlines because Southwest did not provide flights to those cities. So I flew on two different airlines, and both failed...miserably. Not only did they not earn my interest to fly with them again, but they actually did things to effectively "turn me off". The purpose of this article, however, is not to bash those two airlines, but rather to re-focus on how certain missed opportunities could have turned into WOW moments, thus repeat business.

"...customer service is more than just a public relations statement."

Let's start with the first airline. Keep in mind that it may have been the second time that I had flown with them in the last six or seven years. I was on a flight from Baltimore to Chicago and just before the plane door closed, I noticed that over half of the seats were empty. I was in a row with one other passenger, so I decided to move to one of the several empty rows. That way, I could spread out and have ample space to write, read, use my laptop, etc. As I was moving to the adjacent empty row, I heard someone, from a distance, say "No, no, no!" I looked up to see that it was a flight attendant who was speaking to me...plus she was waving her index finger from side to side for added effect. "You have to return to you seat sir!" So, of course, I returned to my seat a bit embarrassed, confused, and annoyed all at the same time. To her credit, she did come to me afterwards to explain why she turned me away from the empty seat.

"Those seats you were going to are premium seats. They have more legroom and there's a charge to sit there." Then she walked away. Ok. I'm sure that she didn't make up that rule or create the flight seat inventory system that allocates "premium seats", but the delivery of the message could have been done more respectfully versus the manner she chose.

On a deeper level, however, why couldn't the airline simply empower their flight attendants to invite passengers to open seats once it had been determined that no more passengers are coming onboard. Hey, maybe I would have fallen in love with the

> *"Such a gesture would have been worth more than any television or newspaper ad."*

extra leg room and told other people about the great seats that the airline has. Or better yet, before I even boarded the plane, the gate agents could have proactively moved passengers to the premium seats once it was clear that those seats would be available. Imagine how impressed passengers would be if the gate agent told some of the fortunate passengers that they were being "upgraded" since there was more than enough room of the flight. Such a gesture would have been worth more than any television or newspaper ad. Customers can always tell when an organization is relationship-driven versus revenue-driven. It was clear that the airline was purely focused on revenue.

On the first leg of another flight, the entire staff seemed like they hated their jobs. Everyone, from the gate agents, to the flight attendants had no smile and barely gave customers any eye contact. When traveling with my baby daughter, I usually check her stroller at the gate versus checking it in as luggage. Since the stroller bag is very large, it, can easily be mistaken for checked luggage by the plane's baggage handlers. So to avoid the potential confusion, I asked the gate attendant for two bag tags versus the customary one tag that is given. That way, the stroller bag could be easier to identify. The gate agent proceeded to roll her eyes at me, mumbled something under her breath and put the two tags on the desk for me to take. Wow.

That same episode could have been re-mixed to get a vastly different outcome. After explaining my situation and asking for the extra bag ticket, the attendant could have:

1. Listened attentively

2. Empathized with the situation (or at least pretended to do so)

3. Given me the tags (or even offered to put them on for me)

4. Wished me a great flight and stated that she hoped that there would be no confusion with my stroller bag during the trip

So there you have it. Two airlines…two missed opportunities to earn my loyalty. It really is a shame, because those airlines, like so many other companies, will look at their financial statements, then notice that revenue and profit are both down. Inevitably, the next steps will usually include a mixture of more advertising, raising prices, laying off staff and charging for things that were previously complimentary.

Instead, companies can win more business by simply re-focusing on the customers' experience. Train and communicate to all staff that the team's mission is to earn the customers' loyalty every day at each touchpoint. Remove restrictions and empower your team to do everything possible to WOW their customers.

"Remove restrictions and empower your team to do everything possible to WOW their customers."

ACTIVITY: Earn and Re-Earn Your Customers' Loyalty

Get with your team and brainstorm various scenarios and how deposits could be made. In short, wow your customers, cherish your customers and honor your customers. They have a choice and you can't take for granted or assume that they will choose you. Adopt an attitude of re-earning your customers' loyalty every day.

_____

_____

_____

_____

_____

_____

_____

_____

_____

_____

_____

_____

_____

30. I Need You

"...it takes a special person to serve others, and it takes an extra special person to serve in health care."

Every patient in every hospital is in a rather strange position. They need the services that the hospital and healthcare providers are giving; but they do not want to be in a situation where they need healthcare in the first place. For the most part, people don't "enjoy" getting sick or injured, but they do. And since this is inevitable, patients reluctantly find themselves fully dependent on people (who they usually don't know). Every patient is saying, "I need you". It is critical for *every* healthcare professional, from physicians to nurses to ER registration clerks to fully understand the moral and emotional responsibility of their work.

Allergy season

My family and I live in the Washington DC metro area, and love it. Before moving there in 2004, I never experienced any asthma problems in my life. Since the move, however, I've developed asthma-like symptoms every year during allergy season. After a few years, it got really bad, so I found a pulmonologist, who diagnosed me with asthmatic bronchitis. He prescribed the appropriate medications to get rid of the ailment. Over the next few years, the same cycle ensued:

allergy season begins...I get sick...I go to the doctor...the Doctor prescribes medication...I feel better...repeat same sequence the following year

Then one year my wife said to me "Why don't you just go see the pulmonologist at the very beginning of allergy season to get the medication. Then you can take the medication every day, as a prophylaxis, until the season ends." Ok, sounds logical, but I immediately thought, "Obviously if that were the case, the doctor would have told me that years ago...right?" So I went to see the doctor and mentioned my wife's suggestion. To my surprise and disappointment, he said "Well, yes, taking the medications pre-emptively is the best route for you to take." What?! Why didn't he tell me that before?

As a patient, *I need you to:*

- *Know that I am a whole person, and not just another transaction:*
- *Make me feel like you are prepared, and looking forward to seeing me.*
- ***Tell me what I don't even know I need to know***...*after all, you are the subject matter expert.*
- *Don't just comply with my requests, but rather look for suggestions to improve my life*
- *Encourage me to follow through on your prescribed actions (medications, etc.)*

Most of all, I need you to care about me, and not just my ability to pay or your ability to cure. I need you to care about my well-being and genuinely want me to be healthy overall.

As I've written previously, it takes a special person to serve others, and it takes an extra special person to serve in healthcare. Healthcare professionals are, in fact, special people. Besides skills, they have the responsibility and privilege to literally improve the life of someone else. Those who fully embrace that responsibility serve with their hearts, and it's a beautiful sight to see. They let love pervade everything they do and say with their patients.

Your ability to connect, sympathize and empathize makes you far more valuable than any check that could ever be written. I need you. Inpatients need you. Outpatients need you. Families need you. Communities need you. Serve with your heart and know that your healthcare job is one of THE most relevant ones the world has ever seen.

ACTIVITY: I Need You

What do your customers need from you? Create a list; ask your team to create a list and then share what you have come up with.

What my customers need from me.